ORLO STRUNK, JR. is professor of psychology and dean of West Virginia Wesleyan College, Buckhannon, West Virginia.

A contributor to such periodicals as *Association of American Colleges Bulletin, The Journal of Pastoral Care, Pastoral Psychology, The Journal of Bible and Religion,* and *Psychological Reports,* he is editor of the book *Readings in the Psychology of Religion,* which contains selections from standard and contemporary literature in the field and a survey of its history.

Dr. Strunk is a graduate of Virginia Wesleyan College (A.B.) and Boston University (S.T.B. and Ph.D.). In addition to his teaching, Dr. Strunk has served as Executive Secretary, Institute of Pastoral Care in Boston, and in 1961 he participated in an international seminar sponsored by the Netherland Universities Foundation, the University of Pittsburgh, and the Intercollegiate Regional Council.

RELIGION
A Psychological Interpretation

Orlo
Strunk, Jr.

RELIGION
A PSYCHOLOGICAL
INTERPRETATION

ABINGDON PRESS • new york • nashville

Psychology, religious

RELIGION: A PSYCHOLOGICAL INTERPRETATION

Copyright © 1962 by Abingdon Press

Library of Congress Catalog Card Number: 62-9386

The excerpts on pages 43 and 57 from Kretch and Crutchfield, *The Theory and Practice of Social Psychology*, © 1948
by McGraw-Hill Book Company, Inc. are used by permission.
    Table on page 58 is from *Youth's Outlook on the Future*,
by Gordon W. Allport and James M. Gillespie. © 1955 by
Random House, Inc. Reprinted by permission.
    The excerpt on page 27 from Hall and Lindzey, *Theories of
Personality*, © 1957 by John Wiley & Sons, Inc. is used by
permission.

SET UP, PRINTED, AND BOUND BY THE
PARTHENON   PRESS,   AT   NASHVILLE,
TENNESSEE, UNITED STATES OF AMERICA

TO MY WIFE

A Mary With Just Enough Martha Traits

PREFACE

The primary purpose of this little book is to introduce the student of religion to a certain psychological framework in which he may raise questions and design research. The framework is not unique or novel in the history of psychology. It has been called phenomenological psychology by some and by others perceptual psychology.

Despite its noble history and adherents, no one in America has attempted to relate this psychological point of view to religious behavior. A majority of our contemporary psychological studies of religion are psychoanalytic or eclectic in their orientation.

No one would argue the point that the rich theoretical framework of psychoanalysis has led to an intense program of research and experimentation in regard to religious behavior. The literature is a stark memorial to this fact.

But there are other potentially fruitful postulational systems. I am convinced that the particular kind of phenomenological or perceptual psychology outlined in this volume is one such system.

I make no claim of completeness in this attempt to view religious behavior perceptually. Indeed, it would be utterly impossible to do justice to this approach without first doing a great deal of founda-

7

tion research. The fact is—and it is an unpleasant fact—*there is practically no research in the psychology of religion which has a distinctively perceptual orientation.*

And this leads us to another salient reason for this volume: To encourage students of religion to design and carry forth research based on the various postulates of the phenomenology outlined in this book.

Thanks and appreciation are due to Arthur W. Combs and Donald Snygg whose book, *Individual Behavior: A Perceptual Approach to Behavior* serves as the bedrock for the present volume. The lucid presentation of the perceptual approach by these two workers already has resulted in wide changes in theoretical positions by psychologists and counselors. I believe their position should also lead to some changes in approach on the part of psychologists of religion.

ORLO STRUNK, JR.

CONTENTS

INTRODUCTION

It is both interesting and significant that many of the great classical psychologists have at some time in their careers become intensely interested in the psychological study of religion. Certainly the father of psychophysics, Gustav Theodor Fechner, may be counted as having something more than a passing interest in religion. Indeed, his classical work, *Elemente der Psychophysik*, had as its *raison d'état* a profound faith in the existence of a spiritual realm. And Fechner's Dr. Mises' excursions are basically religious documents.

Sir Francis Galton also manifested a keen interest in religious phenomena. Though historians of psychology usually view Galton's contributions in the areas of evolutionary conceptualization and individual differences, his interest in religious behavior, such as prayer, has marked historical significance for the psychology of religion (Blacker, 1946; Talbert, 1933).[1]

Even the father of experimental psychology, Wilhelm Wundt, showed interest in religious phenom-

---

[1] Complete bibliographical information of references made in the text may be found at the end of the book under "References."

ena. His *Facts of the Moral Life* (1902) and *Elements of Folk Psychology* (1916) are examples.

In American psychology this propensity toward the study of religion is even more obvious. The great William James may properly be nominated for the title "Father of the Psychology of Religion" on the basis of *The Varieties of Religious Experience* (1902) alone.

And James's contemporary, G. Stanley Hall, first president of the American Psychological Association, showed an intense interest in the psychology of religion. He founded the *American Journal of Religious Psychology and Education*, the first publication specifically devoted to the psychology of religion.

In passing it might be noted that other eminent psychologists in the early days of American psychology made expeditions into the psychology of religion; e.g., Leuba (1912) and Starbuck (1903).

But it is not necessary to look into the history of psychology to observe this somewhat peculiar tendency. In the psychoanalytic stream the movement is even more marked. Freud (1928) showed keen interest in religion, as did Rank (1950), Adler (1933), and Fromm (1950). Jung (1938; 1958), of course, was preoccupied with the problems of religion at the time of his death in 1961.

On the contemporary scene we cannot help noting Gordon W. Allport's (1950) important excursion, and, more recently, the contributions of O. Hobart Mowrer (1959). Current interest is also indicated in special symposia held by the American Psychological Association each year.

These are but a few examples. They naturally lead to the query, Why do psychologists often show intense interest in the psychological study of religion?

Undoubtedly there are many possible answers to our question. Certainly the personal equation cannot be overlooked. Every great psychologist, whether he admits it or not, wants his theories or his system to encompass and explain all behavior.

This would include, of course, highly complex behavior, like religious behavior. Indeed, we might go further and say that religion furnishes the final and most stringent of battlegrounds for the testing of psychological theories. Victory in this complex area assures the adequacy of any truly global psychological system.

Why this is so may aptly be illustrated by making brief references to some of the trends in contemporary psychology itself. The very concepts now gaining popularity are those which find a special place in the religious arena; e.g., the self concept, becoming, self-actualization, growth and change, creativity.

Thirty years ago when classical Behaviorism was on the psychological throne, none of these concepts were acceptable to the average American psychologist. Today, interest in these areas is intense and growing. Each of these concepts has a religious concomitant:

The self concept. The self has found its way back into psychology proper (Allport, 1943; Combs &

Soper, 1957). It is not necessary to indicate the historical relationship between "soul" and "self," since that has been done in great detail by both psychologists (Müller-Freienfels, 1935) and theologians (Niebuhr, 1955). Suffice it is to point out that the very functions psychologists assign to the self are the same as those traditionally considered important by theologians when discussing the soul.

Becoming and Self-Actualization. The switch in psychology from geneticism and reductionism to such concepts as self-actualization (Goldstein, 1939, 1940; Maslow, 1954) and becoming (Allport, 1955) find a clear concomitant in the religious doctrine of perfection.

Growth and Change. Recently many psychologists have made a special point to stress the factors of growth and change, especially in psychotherapy (Rogers & Dymond, 1954). Actually the somewhat optimistic view of man's ability to really change is a relatively new emphasis in psychology proper. In religion, of course, conversion is both a growth and change process, of great interest, we might add, to most of the classical psychologists of religion.

Creativity. Gardner Murphy (1959) and A. Maslow (1954) may be noted as contemporary symbols in the psychologists' attempts to understand the "something new" phenomena. Religion, of course, has always stressed the "new creature" and the "born again" possibility.

Obviously, all of these concepts, plus others, are needed for a proper understanding of religious behavior.

It is, then, no accident that psychologists fre-

quently have turned to the study of religious behavior. In such behavior they have noted the very
unique and complex phenomena which they ultimately hoped to explain with their psychological
theories and facts. When Behaviorism reared its
head it strangled these areas of psychological interest. Now, however, liberalization in conceptualization and methodology has once again opened the
way for the investigation of all kinds of behavior,
both molecular and molar, both simple and complex.

Perhaps, in light of history and in view of our
current interests, the great psychologists of today
will turn their attention to the study of religion.
Such a move would contribute to the building of a
more extensive and meaningful psychological science,
and there is every reason to believe that it would
also lead to a more profound understanding of religion itself.

It is the purpose of this volume to take a step in
this direction. The psychology of religion will be
studied from a specific phenomenological or perceptual point of view. There are, of course, many
phenomenologies (Landsman, 1958), but the one
making up the atmosphere of our study is somewhat unique. We might call it simply perceptual
psychology. This, then, is our major concern: To
interpret religious behavior perceptually.

1
THE PSYCHOLOGICAL STUDY
OF RELIGION

When G. Stanley Hall and his students
turned their psychological sights on the religious
behavior of the individual, there is no doubt that
they held two rather important assumptions. First,
they indicated that psychological frameworks and
methodologies were capable of understanding religious phenomena. Second, they felt that the religious
activities of men were worth trying to understand.
With these two assumptions the classical psychologists of religion met with some success, as the
history of the psychology of religion indicates (Clark,
1958, Ch. 1; Johnson, 1955, Ch. 1; Strunk, 1959,
Ch. 1).

A. The Historical Aspects
Though the classical psychologists of religion met
with limited success, history shows that the vibrant
attempt to understand religion within the psychological framework was an abortive movement.
It staggered under the sterility of Behaviorism, was

partially strangled by a heavily biased theological approach, and experienced a premature and pseudo adulthood from the psychoanalytic school.[1] Its status as a specialized branch of general psychology was practically eliminated. It has since faded into the dynamic and applied field known as pastoral psychology, and was, until recently, in serious danger of losing its autonomy.

Now, however, there are strong indications that the psychology of religion can be reinstated as a legitimate and acceptable field of scientific inquiry. This resurrection is made possible by many contemporary developments in both psychology and theology. Radical conceptual and methodological advancements have been made since the early days of the psychology of religion. The "new psychology" coupled with "liberal theology" offer a congenial atmosphere for the future of the psychology of religion.

B. The Scientific Spirit

We may learn much from the history of the psychology of religion, but if there is one thing we must learn it is to approach our data with a scientific spirit. Frequently the trained psychologist who has developed and nurtured this spirit loses it when his data are in the form of religious events. The history of the psychology of religion contains many examples of this. The student must constantly be on guard at this point.

One way to guard against bias is to be as problem-

[1] The specific factors and implications of these historic trends may be found in (Strunk, 1959).

centered as possible. In psychological science it is quite possible to be method-centered, system-centered, or problem-centered. By method-centered is meant that we have a pet method, and we look for data to treat using this particular method. By system-centered is meant that we have a fairly cogent theoretical system, or we belong to a special "school," and we attempt to fit all observations into this preconceived mold. And by being problem-centered we mean that we look for problems to be tackled and then make careful and intelligent use of appropriate methods and theories.

Though there is nothing intrinsically wrong with being either method-centered or system-centered, the point here is that the complexity of religious phenomena are too diversified and unexplored to be handled adequately by the first two approaches. By viewing religious behavior as a problem area vitally in need of investigation through the use of versatile methodologies and sundry points of view, we cut down on the chances of oversimplification.

Nor is this an argument against developing theoretical frameworks. Indeed, this book is an open attempt to view religious phenomena within the framework of a perceptual or phenomenological psychology. But we must keep in mind what we are doing and appreciate always the possible limitations of our frameworks.

C. What Is the Psychology of Religion?

Though it is not necessary to have a comprehensive definition of the psychology of religion in order to do research, the student might gain a certain perspective if one is offered. So let us define the psychology of religion as *that branch of general psychology which attempts to understand, control, and predict human behavior—both propriate and peripheral—which is perceived as being religious by the individual, and which is susceptible to one or more of the methods of psychological science.*

Our natural objection to such a definition is that we use the term "religious" in defining religion. Though such an objection may be legitimate in a literary sense, it cannot be applied to our perceptual approach, for it is absolutely essential that the definition have its being in the definer.

The psychology of religion is, then, a branch of general psychology in the same sense in which the psychology of personality or the psychology of industry are branches of general psychology. It is not a segment of psychiatry or psychoanalysis, though it may, of course, draw upon these and other specializations for data and hypotheses. The primary function of the psychology of religion is understanding, with control and prediction being rewards of true scientific understanding.

Religious behavior, like all behavior, may be either propriate or peripheral. Propriate behavior refers to that kind of behavior perceived as being personal, warm, and immensely important by the individual, as compared to peripheral behavior which is impersonal, cold, and relatively unimportant (Allport, 1955, pp. 41-58). Both types of behavior are legitimate areas of study for the psychology of religion.

Behavior is here considered, of course, as being much more than motor responses, and includes such things as beliefs and verbalized thoughts and values.

It is necessary that the behavior be perceived as religious by the individual. This perceptual orientation eliminates a great number of weaknesses inherent in the external frame of reference (Combs and Snygg, 1959; Chs. 1 & 2). At times this emphasis on the felt or perceived aspect may have to be inferred from other behavioral events, but, when possible, the perceptual factors should be considered.

Needless to say, the phenomena must be available to at least one of the accepted psychological methods. Quite frequently in the field of the psychology of religion the datum may be of such a nature that the experimental method cannot be used. In such instances, another method or methods may be substituted. Any method which is generally acceptable to psychological science is appropriate. It may be that certain questions in regard to religion are not open to any of the methods of psychological science. When such a problem is presented, the psychology of religion must refer it to another discipline.

The above definition is meant only as an orientational point. It is tentative and open to question. However, the serious student may find it useful as he begins his journey into the psychological study of religion.

D. What Is Religion?

The psychology of religion implies that we are interested in studying *something*. This leads us to the most difficult problem of all, defining our area of concern, the "something" toward which we direct our critical sights.

Recently it has been pointed out that one of the reasons the psychology of religion has not received a great deal of acceptance is that workers have been unable to agree on any one definition (Orr, 1955). Whether such agreement is a necessity for the development of a discipline is certainly a moot question. However, it would do us well to attempt to offer at least a tentative definition for our guidance.

Let us start by suggesting that religion is an organization of cognitive-affective-conative factors, perceived by the individual as being religious in nature, and of being especially appropriate or inappropriate in achieving self-adequacy.

Again it is necessary to remind the reader that contrary to what we might have learned in grade school as to the practice of using the same word in a definition as the word being defined, it is essential, perceptually speaking, to do this since religion is only religion when the perceiver perceives it as such!

Despite the fact that the terms "cognitive," "affective," and "conative" have rich historic connotations and may be considered antiquated by many contemporary psychologists, we have adopted them to give division and direction to our study. We might have used the terms belief-feeling-action to convey our division. The hyphenated nature of this organization is meant to convey the belief that these three aspects are dynamically interrelated. We divide them for didactive purposes and for convenience' sake only.

One of the first criticisms which might be cast at this definition is that it is "too cultural" (Boozer, 1960). Actually what is meant is that it is too *psychological*. We offer no apology at this point. If religion be "something more" than an organization of cognitive-affective-conative factors, then this "something more" transcends the psychological and should be the concern of theology, not psychology.

E. A Psychological Framework

We have already seen that the psychology of religion is too young and its data too complex to approach the subject in any school-centered or system-centered approach. Nevertheless, a general theoretical framework is a useful factor, stimulating research and giving organization to diversified data.

Of course, psychologists of religion have usually operated within the boundaries of some general orientation. At the turn of the twentieth century E. S. Ames (1910) wrote a psychology of religion with a strong functional orientation, and later Trout (1931) approached the subject from a behavioristic bias. More recently W. H. Clark (1958) produced a text heavy with personalistic psychology, and still more recently Paul E. Johnson (1959) revised his text from an interpersonal orientation.

It is good to appreciate and acknowledge frames of reference and postulational systems. Eclecticism is not always—in fact, rarely—a dynamic and stimulating approach (Henle, 1957). Too often eclecticism means a haphazard and disjointed attempt to understand the complex and the puzzling aspects of man's behavior. We can and should remain open to all data and approaches, but we should also have a framework in which we might place the disorganized and often senseless bits of knowledge. This is one reason for having a theoretical framework. And it is best to state that framework from the start (Cunningham, 1956).

The approach to the psychology of religion in this book is strongly perceptual or phenomenological in nature.

It is not necessary at this point in our discussion to spell out the many postulates and assumptions of the perceptual point of view. Actually we will be doing this throughout the rest of this volume. However, there are at least three basic postulates so important that they deserve recognition immediately:[2]

The first is that all behavior, without exception, is completely determined by, and pertinent to, the perceptual field of the behaving organism. By the perceptual field is meant the entire universe, including one's self, as it is experienced by the individual at the instant of action. The psychology of religion is especially concerned with one aspect of this perceptual field, namely that area defined as religious by the behaving organism. Figure 1 illustrates this position. We shall refer to this diagram frequently as we unfold the phenomenological implications of religious behavior.

Secondly, the basic need of human beings is to achieve self-adequacy. We are saying here that all of man's behavior is to be seen as an attempt to main-

[2] These postulates are treated at length by Combs and Snygg (1959, Ch. 3). Also, the reader is referred to a brief but excellent description by Bills (1959).

tain his phenomenal self and to make it more adequate. It must be remembered that by perceived self or phenomenal self is not simply meant the physical self, but the self as perceived. This is an important point, as we shall learn when examining the religious aspects of one's life.

Since we shall make frequent reference to self-adequacy, it is important to know that the adequate personality, perceptually speaking, is one who has achieved a high degree of need satisfaction. Specifically, such people feel generally capable of coping with life, and are quite successful in maintaining and enhancing the self.

Thirdly, man is a self-actualizing creature. Since behavior is a function of perception, individuals must be able to act in reference to their perceptions. In other words, individuals have the capacity for self-actualization; they are not the empty organisms of Locke but the self-starters of Leibnitz (Allport, 1955, Ch. 1).

In this view, behavior is the result not only of external conditions, such as physical or symbolic stimuli, but of internal processes such as ideas, attitudes, and needs.

Besides these three basic assumptions it is rather important that we receive a clear understanding of the type of self system being employed throughout our attempt at interpreting religion.

The word self, of course, has many meanings. In the history of psychology the self (or ego) has been conceived (1) as knower, (2) as object of knowledge, (3) as primordial selfishness, (4) as dominator, (5) as a passive organizer and rationalizer, (6) as a fighter for ends, (7) as one segregated behavioral system among others, (8) as a subjective patterning of cultural values (Allport, 1943).

Our orientation has its roots in Gestalt psychology. The self concept, then, must be understood within the context of a modified field theory.

1. The Perceptual Field

Our use of the term self has its roots in the concept of field (Lewin, 1935; 1936; 1951). Field theory represents an extension of Gestalt psychology. Briefly, the word "field" in physics refers to the gravitational or electrostatic forces surrounding an object and which in turn help to determine the various properties of the object. The example often given is that of a rolling ball. The "behavior" of the ball is determined by both properties inherent in the ball and field forces acting upon it.

Gestalt psychology and later topological psychology have found the field concept helpful in attempting to understand human behavior. Field theory in psychology maintains that the individual exists in an environmental field which is constantly changing; and in order to predict an individual's behavior it is necessary to comprehend both this field and the inner properties of the person.

The assumption is that the perceptual field determines behavior. The perceptual field, as indicated previously, is the entire universe, including the individual, *as it is experienced* by the individual at the instant of action. For all practical purposes, this perceptual field is reality to the person doing the perceiving. This is one of the reasons we must always attempt to discover what the individual perceives; it may not be in accord with the external observer's perceptions, but it and it alone determines behavior.

2. The Phenomenal Self

The perceptual field is the entire universe of awareness. The phenomenal or perceptual self is a portion of the total field which the individual regards as part or characteristic of himself. The phenomenal self is differentiated out of the phenomenal field. Though the phenomenal field determines behavior, the phenomenal self is a special part of this total field and has special significance for the individual. The phenomenal self is a doer as well as an object. As Combs says:

It . . . is quite possible, indeed is characteristic of everything we know of in the world of science; namely, that every organization is both composed of certain parts while at the same time it affects other organizations upon which it impinges. Thus, a rock is made up of certain molecules and is thus a product. It also, by its very existence, has an effect upon the world around it or upon the world in which it rests, and is thus also a process or a dynamic. In the same way, the self is composed of perceptions concerning the individual and this organization of perceptions in turn has vital and important effects upon the behavior of the individual. [Hall and Lindzey, 1957, p. 470.]

There are, of course, hundreds of ways in which an individual perceives himself. At one moment Mr. Simmons might perceive himself as a good father

who loves and supports his family. At another moment he might perceive himself as the best golf
player in his Rotary Club. But the unique way in
which Mr. Simmons organizes his self perceptions
makes up the phenomenal self. The phenomenal
self, then, is the organization or pattern of all these
perceptions which the individual refers to as "I"
or "me."

The phenomenal self is not a mere conglomeration
or addition of isolated concepts of self, but a patterned interrelationship or Gestalt of all of these. It
is the individual as he seems from his own vantage
point. [Combs & Snygg, 1959, p. 126.]

3. The Self Concept

Just as it is possible to differentiate out of the
perceptual field the phenomenal self, so is it possible
to differentiate out of both the perceptual field and
the phenomenal self the self concept. The self concept represents an organization of perceptions which
seem especially important to the individual. He cannot conceive of himself without these aspects.

In referring to these very special perceptual aspects
we shall use Allport's term, *propriate*. Propriate states
and processes are perceived as being especially warm,
close, and personal by the individual. Propriate states
and processes include those aspects of personality
which make for inward unity (Allport, 1955, pp.
41-56).

The general usefulness of propriate properties may
be found in the distinction the concept helps to
draw between intimate behavioral events, those having importance for the individual, and behavioral

events which are relatively unimportant to the individual.

These three concepts, then—the phenomenal field, the phenomenal self, and the self concept—should be kept in mind as we examine the domain of religion.

Figure 1 may be of assistance to the reader in attempting to grasp the self system being employed in this discussion.

F. Religion and the Self System

The total self system is made up of a variety of factors. These factors include experiences of all kinds. It is quite possible to acknowledge a multitude of factors which go into the formation of a self system. Indeed, all perceptions ever made, either clearly or vaguely, go into the construction of the self. Included in the "I" or the "me" are all experiences ever experienced. Some events, of course, are more important than others. The degree of importance may be determined by many things. For example, the intensity of the experience, the duration of the experience, the circumstances surrounding the experience, and a host of other factors.

Our specific concern is with those factors of a religious nature. Very often the religious factor may be easily identified. An experience of prayer, for example, may safely be classified as a religious event or factor. The pray-er himself would agree. The observer would also agree.

But there are factors or behavioral events which may be less obvious. In such cases, we must take seriously the judgment of the behaver; if he says his behavior is religious, it is religious.

If a Communist views his belief system as essentially religious, then it must be understood and appreciated in this light. Our opinion may differ, but, psychologically, we are observing the *religious* behavior of the Communist.

Because the individual's perceptions are so important, it is necessary for us to get some idea of how a self system is formed and how the religious factors are defined and made part of that system.

1. The Beginnings of the Self System

Birth undoubtedly marks a significant developmental point in the formation of the self concept. It has been postulated that in early infancy the organism cannot distinguish itself from its environment. Only the most intense kind of stimuli elicit responses from the infant. The newly born organism is unable to differentiate with precision. Yet differentiation is necessary for identification purposes. This is one of the reasons why some psychologists insist that a neonate is without personality, and why some psychologists of religion insist that in early childhood religion is impossible (Allport, 1950; Ch. 2). After all, religion must be learned (differentiated) and with the differentiation process nearly zero, religious factors cannot possibly be perceived, let alone internalized.

But even before birth the organism has a psychological field. It may be vague (undifferentiated) and hectic, but it is a field with forces and an interrelationship of dynamic factors. The exact nature of these early and highly vague perceptions has remained a mystery to us.

When the child is cast out into the world of stimuli the raw materials for the development of the self system begin to make their marks. At first the newborn infant's perceptions are fuzzy, and the result is that its behavior is gross and seemingly random. However, it is not long before sharper differentiation begins to take hold. In the early months of development, the child shows a remarkable capacity to make perceptions more precise, and with the sophistication of differentiations comes more specific behavior.

One of the first perceptual events of marked significance is the discovery of the self. At first the infant does not make a clear distinction between self and environment. However, after a long and complicated process of trial and error behavior, the child begins to make a distinction between the "me" and the "not me." The child's contacts with objects and persons soon define himself. Some children are able to make a clear distinction between self and others at a very early age. Once this crucial step is made, it is not long before the phenomenal self takes clear shape.

It is no longer a matter now of making the distinction, but of adding values to the discriminations. It is not only "me" and "not me" but "good me" or "bad me" and "good you" and "bad you."

When this stage is reached, perceptual processes become highly complex and social laden. The definition of self will now be greatly influenced by family relationships and cultural influences. Later we shall see how perceptions of parents may be a salient factor in developing religious concepts. Specific environmental factors, such as geographical situation, may actually be internalized and partially determine the child's idea of God (Takenaka, 1939).

At present we know little about the specific ways in which modern children learn to perceive themselves. Equally true is the fact that we have very little concrete information on how children first perceive religious objects, though there is no convincing reason why the psychologist of religion cannot investigate children's concepts of God, Christ, Church, the Sacraments, the Ministry.

Recently one worker made an interesting study of the specific ways in which Negro children became aware of the fact that they were Negro. This worker asked elementary school children in the South the question: "When did you first discover that you were a Negro?" There were, of course, many reasons, with verbal information from parents and peers high on the list. This information, once accepted (internalized), contributed greatly to the change and formation of the phenomenal self. And, obviously, the analysis of the varied answers given to the question led to an abundant reservoir of hypotheses and inferences.

Similar studies designed by the psychologist of religion in his search for an understanding of early religious influences are desperately needed.

2. The Self and Religious Objects

The phenomenal self consists of a variety of factors. Actually religious factors do not present themselves until quite late in childhood. It is true that a very young child may go through the motions of religious behavior. Allport (1950, p. 29) tells of a four-year-old who had learned to say his nightly prayers before a religious picture. Visiting in a house other than his own, he found no religious picture available. He did, however, find a copy of the *Saturday Evening Post*, and using the cover picture, he was able to say his prayers.

In this case the conative (action) aspect of religion is present, but there is little in the way of cognition (knowledge) and affection (feeling). In a sense, such behavior can hardly be called religious, though it certainly may have deep religious implications. Frequently such behavior represents the beginning of the development of the religious aspect of the phenomenal self. At first, however, it can hardly be more than social behavior, vague effective states, and egocentric strivings.

Fahs (1930) has done an admirable job of emphasizing the importance of these early pseudo-religious and nonreligious experiences. After analyzing the recollections made by graduate students of their earliest childhood "religion," this worker concludes

that the most influential philosophy, bordering on religion, that any of us lives by, is one of his own making, long since buried in the unconscious along with his first dreams and first wishes and fears. In fact, the proposition is ventured that the process of creating our religion began for each of us the day of our birth. Before we were conscious of what we were doing, while emotions swayed the outreachings of inherited impulses, we were setting our goals. On the basis of the feelings which the adults about us stirred within us by their attentions or lack of attentions, we drew perhaps the most significant conclusions we have ever drawn in our lives. . . . In the early months we have determined upon the color of glass through which we look out on life, and every experience that came to us was tinted by it. . . . If, as the years passed, this universe grew to include God, either we became willing to remake and enlarge our picture, or God was fitted into the picture we had already painted.

What is being said here is that latter religious perceptions are determined by previous experiences of a nonreligious nature. At a very early age, the child is unable to make *religious* perceptions since he has not developed a differentiating process of adequate sophistication. Nevertheless, he has all kinds of experiences which leave their mark and which create perceptual inclinations. These propensities—including temperament and the psychological experiences of infancy—may well color later perceptions of religious objects.

Perhaps the most conspicuous illustration of the way in which early perceptions determine later perceptions is the psychoanalytic hypothesis that the God concept is formed by the projection of attitudes and feelings toward one's earthly father into a pattern that could be thought of as a supernatural father.[3] Ernst Jones (1944), psychoanalyst, pre-

[3] This discussion draws heavily on work done by Nelson and Jones (1957) and my own research (Strunk, 1959a).

sented the doctrine well when he wrote that "the religious life represents a dramatization on a cosmic plane of the emotions, fears, and longings which arose in the child's relation to the parents."

In order to test this hypothesis, Nelson and Jones (1957) constructed an instrument, based on the Q-Technique (Stephenson, 1953), to measure the relationship between religious concepts and parental concepts.[4] A list of sixty statements was constructed, each statement so worded that it could be used to complete any one of the following sentences: "When I think of God I . . .;" "When I think of Jesus I . . .;" "When I think of Father I . . .;" "When I think of Mother I. . . ."

Sixteen persons were then asked to sort the sixty statements according to a standard procedure. Nelson and Jones discovered a greater relationship between the nature of deity concepts (God and Jesus) and those of Mother concept than between deity concepts and concept of Father. Though relationships were frequently significant, they were not in the direction of Freud's theory.

Strunk (1959) then did a similar study, giving the same statements to twenty religiously oriented persons. In this study a significant relationship between God and Father concepts was obtained, supporting the general Freudian thesis. However, the relationship between God and Father was found to be the least significant of the deity-parental combinations!

[4] The student interested in the rationale and procedure of the Q-Technique should consult Stevenson (1953), and Nelson and Jones (1957).

Though this research does not give great support to the specific Freudian theory, it does illustrate the tendency for people to perceive religious objects as they perceive parental objects. The early childhood perceptions, though perhaps now relatively undifferentiated (unconscious), may still be quite influential in determining contemporary peceptions of religious objects.

Of course there is nothing particularly novel or startling about this since we do know that perceptions are determined by many factors which are not throughly differentiated, including such obvious things as physiological processes and social value systems. These, however, may all be seen in terms of our desire for self-adequacy, the physiological represented on one level and social values on another. Those things which satisfy our need for self-adequacy are *valued*. What we are saying here is that in the early stages of development those objects which satisfy this need are rarely if ever perceived as being religious. Nevertheless, the ways in which self-adequacy is obtained sets the stage for later perceptions of the kind called *religious* by the perceiver.

SUMMARY

We have tried in this chapter to spell out our presuppositions and biases. The history of the psychology of religion teaches us that it is essential to maintain a scientific approach, to be as problem-centered as possible in our research, and to develop a general frame of reference in which to work.

We have defined the psychology of religion as

that branch of general psychology which attempts to understand, control, and predict human behavior —both propriate and peripheral—which is perceived as being religious by the individual, and which is susceptible to one or more of the methods of psychological science. And we have defined religion as an organization of cognitive-affective-conative factors, perceived by the individual as being religious in nature, and of being especially appropriate or inappropriate in achieving self-adequacy.

Our psychological orientation is primarily to be phenomenological or perceptual in nature. There are at least three basic postulates of this perceptual approach: (1) All behavior, without exception, is completely determined by, and pertinent to, the perceptual field of the behaving organism; (2) the basic need of human beings is to maintain and enhance the perceived self (self-adequacy); and (3) man is a self-actualizing creature.

The self system, so essential to our perceptual approach, affords a convenient context in which to view religious beliefs. The *perceptual field* is the entire universe, including the individual, as it is experienced by the individual at the instant of action. The *phenomenal self* is a portion of this total field which the individual regards as part or characteristic of himself. The *self concept* is differentiated out of the phenomenal self and is noted for its very personal and important meaning to the persons.

This self system is made up of a variety of factors, but the specific factor of concern in our study is that which is called religious by the individual. In the early development of the self system religious factors per se are lacking. Nevertheless, very early perceptions are important in understanding religious behavior in that latter religious perceptions are frequently determined by early experiences of a non-religious nature.

2
COGNITIVE ASPECTS OF
RELIGION

Needs and perceptions are psychological units which may tell us much about religious behavior. But it is also profitable to study higher order phenomena, such as beliefs and attitudes. It is certainly in these areas that religion operates a great deal of the time, and it is in this higher order sphere that religion invests its meaning. This is obvious when we note how very often the mention of belief brings with it religious associations and discussion. We know that there are also political beliefs, economic beliefs, and educational beliefs, but it is usually not of these that we think when the subject of belief is mentioned. Religious beliefs are inherent in the study of religious phenomena.

The psychological study of religious beliefs can only note whence come beliefs and how they function (Lawton, 1930). It cannot determine the validity or falsity of a belief. This is a function of other disciplines, especially logic and theology. For psychology the importance of a belief lies in the fact that an individual believes such-and-such to be true and may act accordingly. If, for instance, as Jung (1938, p. 3) points out, the psychologist of religion turns his attention to the doctrine of the virgin birth, he is not concerned as to the validity of such a belief. The virgin birth is psychologically true because the belief is held by some persons.

This may appear to be a disquieting position in which to operate but the history of the psychology of religion reveals that to do otherwise leads to interminable argumentation and ineffectual speculation.

A. Need as a Convenient Construct

The concept of need has a long and complex place in the history of psychology. Essentially, it represents a cumulative concept constructed atop such words as instinct, drive, and incentive (Boring, 1950, p. 716).

Briefly, a need may be defined as the lack of something which, if present, would tend to further the welfare of the organism or of the species, or to facilitate its usual behavior (English & English, 1958, p. 338). There are many need systems and theories in psychology proper. Murray (1938), for example, has constructed a psychology of personality within a need context, as has Maslow (1954) in his theory of a hierarchy of needs.

Despite the popularity of need theories, the concept has been severely criticized. Indeed, the various need theories have experienced the same critical attacks as the instinct theories did during the early part of the twentieth century. For one of the difficulties of any need theory is the task of classifying and numbering needs. Agreement among theorists is difficult to find. Murray, for example, recognizes over thirty needs, and Maslow describes a minimum of six. Needs may range anywhere from one to hundreds. One may have a need to survive, suck on a pipe, wink at pretty girls, watch baseball, ad infinitum.

The problem of classification and numbering of instincts led psychologists to abandon the concept until recently when some noble attempts have been made toward reinstatement (Oppenheimer, 1958). The same fate may overtake the need concept, if it is not handled carefully. In hope of avoiding this, Combs and Snygg (1959) recently postulated the existence of a single need, namely, the need for adequacy.

These authors root their hypothesis in the concept of man as a being continuous with the universe. The maintenance of organization is a principle implicit in the universe generally. Man, as part of the universe, is engaged in a similar task of maintaining organization. There is, of course, a physiological aspect involved in the organization tendency, but man does not live in a physical world alone.

The universe in which he lives and maintains his organization is a universe of ideas, values, societies, and people. Man, furthermore, is as much a part of these aspects of his universe as he is of its physical aspects. Like the larger organization of which he is part and the smaller organization of which he is product, he maintains the organization he is. The self man seeks to maintain is not just his physical body but the self of which he is aware, the self he has come to consider his personality, that unique being known as John Jones or Sally Smith. This self is called the perceived, or phenomenal, self. [Combs & Snygg, 1959, p. 43.]

This phenomenal or perceived self is a key concept in our approach to the psychological understanding of religious behavior. For all behavior, we must remember, is an attempt to achieve adequacy, to maintain and enhance the perceived self. Religious behavior, we hope to show, is one way of achieving self-adequacy.

B. Religious Beliefs

Just as defining what is meant by "needs" is a difficult exercise so also is the word "belief." In attempting to define belief we shall emphasize the perceptual and cognitional aspects of the term. Warren (1934) has defined belief as the acceptance of a principle, doctrine, statement, and so forth, on the basis of evidence which is assumed to be adequate. This is a good general definition, stressing the cognitive aspect of a belief as it does. Krech and Crutchfield's definition, though similar, is, however, more specific and functional: "A belief is an enduring organization of perceptions and cognitions about some aspect of the individual's world" (Krech & Crutchfield, 1948, p. 150).

At this point we are apt to sense that there is a difference between the statements "I believe in God" and "I have faith in God." It is important that this sense of distinction be made clear and explicit. Beliefs are concerned primarily with matters which the individual perceives as being verifiable.

Those beliefs of the individual which he himself recognizes as intrinsically unverifiable are referred to as matters of *faith*. He believes (i.e., has faith) that an omnipresent, all-knowing God exists, although he himself may never, in the very nature of his conceptions about God, "prove" the validity of his belief to his own satisfaction. [Krech & Crutchfield, 1948, p. 166.]

If we recognize this primary distinction between belief and faith, we are able to understand why it is that beliefs are less complex than is faith. Faith is highly propriate in nature, i.e., it is warm and close to the individual. This is not necessarily true of beliefs. Indeed, beliefs may be without any high degree of affect, whereas faith is always a matter of self-investment.

It is, of course, exceedingly difficult to make a sharp dichotomy between belief and faith in real life. This seems especially true with regard to religious beliefs, which are often held with strong tenacity. Some years ago, Thouless (1935) performed an experiment in which he presented to a large group of subjects some statements on religious and non-religious questions, asking them to indicate the degree of certainty with which they believed or disbelieved these statements. The experimenter also asked the same subjects to estimate the probability of various chance events connected with the tossing and the drawing of cards. Thouless' results indicated that religious beliefs tend to be held to or to be rejected with a high degree of conviction. This seems to suggest that religious beliefs are especially propriate in nature, though the belief itself is intellectual or cognitive in nature.

Thouless suggests that people should hold to religious beliefs with less tenacity. But, really, this is a somewhat hollow suggestion, for religious beliefs are usually intrinsically unverifiable and, therefore, represent matters of faith. Though beliefs as such may be stated and responded to by the individual, religious beliefs usually are of such a nature that they tend to be converted into matters of faith. In terms of our perceptual orientation, religious beliefs tend to be *internalized* and made part of our perceived self.

C. Beliefs and Needs

The statement that needs determine beliefs is a simple and sovereign principle which contains enough truth to make it an important consideration. There is surely a sense in which beliefs, especially religious beliefs, are instrumental behaviors which serve to relieve the tensions which are called needs.

An individual may, for example, have a strong need for safety and may partially satisfy this need by internalizing the belief that he is one of God's children, cared for, watched over, and protected.

The individual's basic need, however, is to maintain and enhance the perceived self. One facet of this need is the attempt to make meaning out of life's experiences. This subsidiary need for meaning and organization is partially met by beliefs.

Ordinarily, there are plenty of beliefs around to handle the average person's life situations. Through the socialization process, the child and adolescent internalizes orthodox beliefs from parents and institutions. As needs arise, the child finds ready-made beliefs especially suited for specific needs. Allport (1951) has called this stage of belief the "verbal realism" stage. The child accepts words as facts. From the external frame of reference, these beliefs are usually quite irrational and authoritarian in nature, but, generally, they contribute to the child's need for adequacy. As the intensity and complexity of life are met, however, old beliefs very often prove inefficient and naïve and new beliefs must be formulated and integrated.

This general principle is well illustrated in the case of the religious group known as Christian Scientist. Religiously oriented persons, especially those who believe in a good God, are frequently greatly troubled by the presence of sickness and suffering. The desire to explain this seemingly inconsistent belief in God—a desire originating in one's own search for an adequate self—has led the founder of this religion to formulate a theoretical system which in actuality denies the reality of suffering, placing the entire matter on the shoulders of the believer (or unbeliever).

Using the method of content analysis, England (1954) has shown that the beliefs (faith) of this cult quite often do lead to cures of physical ailments. And in a similar study by Strunk (1955), it was shown that the Christian Scientist's *Weltan-schauung* is capable of rising to all occasions, explaining simple and minor "bad habits" as well as war worries and cosmic inconsistencies—and in terms which apparently satisfy a goodly number of the sect's membership.

It is probably true, however, that such a conspicuous and startling search for meaning is exceptional in most cultures. As Krech and Crutchfield (1948, p. 154) remind us, "Beliefs grow and change only to the minimal extent that is called for by the exigencies of the individual's immediate situation in life."

The chaplain in the hospital is soon made aware of this general observation. Below is an excerpt from a typical interview with a patient which points up the fact that new experiences often demand new beliefs:

CHAPLAIN: I'm Chaplain Johnson. I've stopped by to see how you are making out.

PATIENT: That's very nice of you. I'm very glad you wanted to see me. I'm not feeling as well as I thought I would be.

CHAPLAIN: It takes a while sometimes. But you seem much better than you were.

PATIENT: Well I'm not in the oxygen tent any more; but I'm still so weak.

CHAPLAIN: I see.

PATIENT: It's so hard to understand it all. So many terrible things happen. There seems to be no reason for it. It's all a mystery.

CHAPLAIN: There are so many mysterious things in the world that it seems beyond our power to understand them.

PATIENT: Yes, that's it. So many good people suffer. They lose their health, their money, and there seems to be no justice in it.

CHAPLAIN: Hmmm.

PATIENT: It seems like we can't understand this universe. It seems like a great mystery lies at the end of it and it's not for us to know.

CHAPLAIN: You feel as though you can't understand what the world is all about.

PATIENT: Yes. What do you think the universe is all about? Do you think you know something about the meaning of the world?

CHAPLAIN: It is difficult to say; it requires a great deal of thought and faith.

PATIENT: But when these terrible things happen, how do you find the faith and strength to endure them? *How?*

This patient is searching for beliefs which will meet her present situation. Her old set of beliefs is now under fire, and she is beginning to wonder if it is adequate for her new position. She is demanding that the clergyman give her a new and more adequate schema of beliefs.

Changes in beliefs are to be expected, especially when the individual is a growing person. The extension of the self, the involvement in new situations, is demanding and complex. In his constant attempt to create an adequate self, new beliefs must be found, must be organized, must be internalized. To fail to do this, either with clear differentiating or vague differentiating (unconscious), leads to arrested growth and abnormalities. The pathology of religion reveals that religious persons who doggedly retain childish beliefs in the face of powerful and highly complex situations often are led into bigotry and other states considered "abnormal" by society.

This functional significance of beliefs, which we have stressed above, should point up an important warning, namely, that we dare not explain contemporary beliefs simply on genetic grounds. There is a persistence and stability to most beliefs, as our definition has indicated, but the ways in which we choose to maintain and enhance our perceived self vary greatly in the socialization process. The belief that God is a stern father who portions out rewards and punishments in a judgmental way might satisfy the adolescent's search for self-adequacy. But in adulthood the same individual might cast aside this belief as being ineffective. Or, perhaps just as likely, he might strengthen this belief in an effort to make sense of his world. The belief, in other words, might have its roots in childhood, but now it is held to for quite other reasons. The basic need of self-adequacy is still present but the *perception* of the belief may have changed tremendously in the intervening years.

Though the need-belief principle outlined above may appeal to our desire for parsimonious explanations, we must be very cautious in using it in any global way. Any belief may, on the surface, serve different ends; yet different needs, if a multineed system is proposed, may lead to the same belief! Thus it is that the seemingly simple and sovereign principle of needs-beliefs, like most simple and sovereign theories, leaves much to be desired. It might help us in research design and even in explanatory analysis, but it is a slippery and questionable principle when used in a one-to-one setting.

It is better to assume our one basic need, that of self-adequacy, and then attempt to discover the various ways religion factors, such as beliefs, may be functionally related to the maintenance and enhancement of the perceived self.

D. Function of Religious Beliefs

The primary and salient function of religious beliefs is to achieve self-adequacy. We believe only that which in one way or another maintains or enhances our perceived self. But this must not be viewed as a simple and easy explanation, for the precise ways in which religious beliefs fulfill this function are complex and little known. Indeed, one of the major tasks facing the psychology of religion is to describe exactly how beliefs may satisfy our need for adequacy. To date we have little empirical information on this problem.

Despite the lack of research, however, there are several principles and research findings which demonstrate the function of religious beliefs in the process of self-enhancement and maintenance.

It would be quite possible to illustrate the functional significance of religious beliefs by quoting extensively from anthropological sources and from the science of religion usually referred to as the history of religion. Many religious beliefs, especially in primitive societies, directly or indirectly satisfy specific biological needs. Dunlap's volume (1946), for example, is devoted almost exclusively to showing the close relationship existing between biological needs and religious practices.

All of these functions of religion may be accurate, if not exhaustive. Psychology, however, has long since moved beyond the simple drives and needs of elementary existence. Man is a social animal, and many of his motives are social and highly complex. These "higher factors" and the way religious beliefs are related to them constitute a significant area of investigation.

No matter our peculiar outlook on this theoretical issue, there is little doubt any more as to the *relationship* between beliefs and behavior. The crucial question is, Exactly what is the nature of these relationships? Why, for example, does a man insist that he believes in the brotherhood of man and yet behave in ways which seem to indicate that he does not hold to that belief?

The answer to such questions, though inconclusive, compels us to examine the internalization process itself, for a belief, it appears, influences behavior only when *perceived* by a person; and the degree of influence appears to be directly related to the intensity of the internalization process.

E. Intensity of Religious Beliefs

One of the primary assumptions of the perceptionist is that an individual behaves in ways which are consistent with his view of the world. As Bills (1959, pp. 55-56) notes, "When man believed that the world was flat, he avoided the edges. When he believed that demons and devils caused disease, he attempted to drive them out with bad odors and loud noises."

Despite the seeming soundness of this thesis, the literature indicates some problems in the belief-behavior relationship. It is, for example, quite impossible to predict accurately behavioral events simply by knowing an individual's belief schema. Frequently, specific actions do not follow specific beliefs.

The problem is demonstrated in this assertion made by a distraught counselee: "All my life I've believed that I should love my enemies, but I don't."

This problem may be approached in several ways, but one of the most creative has been that of indicating that religion may manifest itself on a continuum from little or no intensity to great intensity. There have been several attempts to set up divisions or levels, the most recent being that of Clark's *primary, secondary,* and *tertiary* religion (Clark, 1958, Ch. 2). Primary religion corresponds to religion found in individuals described by William James as those "for whom religion exists not as a dull habit but as an acute fever." Secondary religion represents the "dull habit" kind, despite, perhaps, an initial primary experience. And tertiary religious behavior refers to religious routine or convention accepted on the authority of someone else.

This division is helpful. If we should ask any of

these persons to respond to the question, "Do you believe in God?", we would undoubtedly get a unanimous "yes." But the resultant behavior may vary tremendously among the three types of religion. Unfortunately, there are few studies in the literature which detect and recognize the *intensity* of religious beliefs.

As we have indicated, Clark's distinction is helpful. But the content of these three "types" of religion is left pretty much to external observation. It is also possible to visualize levels or degrees of religious beliefs in terms of the self system itself and to make a simple recognition of intensity with the concepts of *propriate* and *peripheral*.

1. Peripheral Religious Beliefs

The diagram in Figure 1 gives a crude but helpful picture of the self system. The area labeled "phenomenal field" contains many factors which the individual is aware of, but which may never truly become important to him.

Religious beliefs may rest in this outer fringe, as illustrated by the black area in Figure 2. Though these beliefs are contained in the psychological field of the individual and may determine behavior, they are peripheral in that they remain away from the self concept, that organization of perceptions which seems especially important to the individual.

Any set of religious beliefs may remain in this fringe area. The individual with such "fringe religiosity" frequently participates in religious activities, but his self concept is not saturated with religious beliefs. Indeed, he may do a surprisingly good job of perceiving religious beliefs in such a way as to never become too involved in them. He perceives religious beliefs, and they help him achieve self-adequacy, but he might well do without them. If we should ask this person to describe his self concept by ranking descriptive adjectives, the religious adjective would not be placed at the top.

2. Propriate Religious Beliefs

Previously we made reference to propriate religious behavior. Our proposed definition of the psychology of religion contains the term. Propriate refers to behavior perceived as being especially warm, personal, and important by the individual.

Unlike peripheral religious beliefs, propriate beliefs have been deeply internalized. Indeed, the internalization may go to the very core of the self concept. Figures 3 and 4 give a visual representation of this internalization process.

Here beliefs become more than static verbalizations. They have been integrated and represent an actual part of the self system, perhaps even an important aspect of the self concept itself.

Seen developmentally, religious beliefs in childhood are often peripheral in nature. Even religious practices may be perfunctory events, having little importance and meaning for the individual. Later, perhaps, these same events may be embraced, given meaning and significance, and actually becoming a part of one's self. On the other hand, of course, these beliefs may in adolescence or later years be relegated to the periphery. The direction will de-

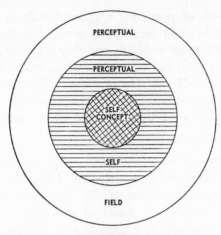

Figure I

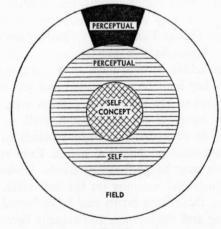

Figure II

pend on the perceived success the beliefs have in the search for self-adequacy.

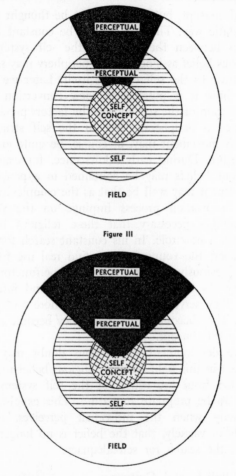

Figure III

Figure IV

F. Dynamic Character of Religious Beliefs

This distinction between peripheral and propriate religion in terms of location in the self system is a useful concept, but it should not be thought of in any static way. There is or may be constant interaction between the layers of the self system. A religious belief assigned to the periphery may slowly penetrate to the self concept itself. Later we shall note how it is possible to view conversion as a penetration of the self concept by factors previously assigned a peripheral place in the self structure.

This movement may, of course, be quite gradual in nature. During early adolescence, for example, religious beliefs may be contained in a peripheral area. But it may well be that as the complexities of the socialization process impinge on the youth, it becomes necessary that these religious beliefs take on a new role. In his constant search for self-adequacy, the youngster may find real use for beliefs previously held to with only perfunctory intensity. As these beliefs are rarefied and internalized, they serve the individual in more and more ways. They become important. They become a part of the self concept.

The development of religious doubt may also be seen in this light. Here a religious belief may be expelled from the center of the self system and cease to be propriate in nature. This expulsion is necessary when the individual perceives, either clearly or vaguely, that the belief is no longer useful in the search for self-adequacy.

G. Beliefs and Culture

We have up to this point given the impression that beliefs are the result of man's need for an adequate self and that these beliefs are pretty much ready made and easily available. We are prone to assume that one's beliefs are more or less handed down from authority figures, such as parents, state, church, and so forth. It is of course axiomatic that we are greatly influenced by our culture. The fact most Americans are Christians and not Mohammedans is testimony to this observation. But just *how* these cultural influences determine beliefs is a difficult and as yet unsolved problem. It would be pleasant, from the scientific point of view, if we could find a pat one-to-one relationship between specific beliefs and specific cultural influences. But it appears that the task is exceedingly complex.

The relationship between the influence of cultural agencies and the resulting beliefs and attitudes is so complex that in some instances the effect of the parent's influence can be seen to account for the rise of a belief or attitude that is in opposition to the parent's belief. [Krech & Crutchfield, 1948, p. 182.]

Once this is said, however, we must admit the importance of cultural influences in shaping beliefs. To date there have been very few cross-cultural studies of religious beliefs.

However, Gillespie and Allport (1955) have recently completed such a study which is both significant and pioneering in nature. These workers, using an "autobiography of the future" and a questionnaire, investigated students' attitudes in ten different countries. One of the questions asked was,

Do you feel that you require some form of religious orientation or belief in order to achieve a fully mature philosophy of life? Table 1 shows the responses to this question.

TABLE 1

PERCENTAGE OF STUDENTS EXPRESSING A NEED FOR RELIGION

| | NUMBER | | YES | | No OR DOUBTFUL | |
	Men	Women	Men	Women	Men	Women
United States	591	188	64	77	36	23
New Zealand	73	52	53	69	47	31
South Africa						
English	15	13	73	69	27	31
Afrikaner	25	40	80	90	20	10
Bantu	35	13	49	62	51	38
Egypt	31	32	68	59	32	41
Mexico	111	104	54	53	46	47
France	108	24	56	42	44	58
Italy	40	37	95	92	5	8
Germany	19	11	84	73	16	27
Japan	72	118	33	72	67	28
Israel	26	10	27	40	73	60

Though the smallness of this sample prevents us from making any conclusive generalizations, it is interesting to note that there are marked differences in the response to this question. For example, one aspect is the obvious laxity of religious orientation manifested in the Israel sample. Ordinarily, we might assume that the cradle of several great religions would give quite another picture. Though we are not free to interpret Table 1 on purely cultural grounds, it does give us some indications of the important role of cultured influences.

Our interpretation of these data is that though the young Israelites need to maintain and enhance their phenomenal selves, they are, generally speaking, finding ways other than religious to do this. Possibly the military atmosphere or the political facets of Israel at the time of the survey may be furnishing the youth better ways to achieve self-adequacy. Or, perhaps equally important, the very historic vicissitudes may be perceived negatively by the youth. Again, an indication of the importance of *perceptions* rather than "objective factors."

Changes in beliefs may also be accountable in terms of cultural change, though, again, our evidence is meager. Dudycha (1934, 1950) has done an interesting study in this regard. In 1930 this worker administered a battery of religious propositions to college freshmen, asking them to indicate their belief or disbelief in each proposition. Table 2 shows the results of this initial inquiry.

TABLE 2

Belief	Percentage Believing
1. Ten Commandments should be obeyed	98
2. Existence of God	96
3. Divinity of Jesus Christ	93
4. Existence of the soul	92
5. Christ died to save sinners	90

Then, twenty years later, Dudycha administered the same battery of propositions to the college freshmen of that year. In this way it was possible to compare the religious beliefs of 266 freshmen listed in 1930 with the beliefs of the 852 freshmen in 1950. The results of this single study seem to indicate that "the degree of acceptance and rejection of religious belief is very similar for the 1930 and 1949 college freshmen tested. Both groups indicate greatest belief in the same religious propositions and least belief in essentially the same propositions.

. . . In the light of these results, limited as they are, it does not seem that the events of the last two decades have had a marked effect on the religious beliefs of college freshmen" (Dudycha, 1950, p. 169).

Of course, the 1930 freshmen needed these religious beliefs in order to achieve self-adequacy, but so also did the 1950 freshmen. In this case, it would appear, cultural factors did not change enough to effect beliefs.

It is also quite possible that the 1950 students' beliefs have changed radically from the 1930 sample, but their use of verbal symbols has not. That is, the 1950 students may respond to the item on sin exactly as did the 1930 students, *but mean something entirely different;* they still use the word "sin" but the meaning for them is quite different than the meaning held by the earlier group.

It would help us a great deal if we could give this battery of propositions to the *same individuals* in 1950 as was done in 1930, for certainly developmental factors contribute greatly to what is believed.

Lundeen and Caldwell (1930), for instance, in comparing the beliefs of high school seniors with those of college students, found some significant differences. These two workers presented certain types of "unfounded beliefs" to 918 high school students and to 294 college students. In comparing the scores, it was discovered that education and experience apparently tend to reduce belief in such items, since college students showed less belief than high school seniors and were influenced by such beliefs to a lesser degree.

Such studies in belief are greatly needed. From the few bits of research done to date, we have a general idea that beliefs do change with the maturation of the individual and that "the times" have little effect on what is believed, except, of course, in terms of great periods of time.

It is equally apparent that beliefs are enduring organizations of perceptions and cognitions. It may well be, as Stephens (1951) has suggested, that though specific doctrines (e.g., virgin birth of Christ, literal heaven and hell, and so forth) are believed less and less, the abstract religious beliefs (e.g., fellowship of man, eternal governing principle, and so forth) are held to with a relatively great degree of stability. All of this points out once more the complexity and interrelationships between cultural factors and beliefs.

The reader will recognize at once that it would be quite possible and legitimate to study beliefs from a cultural orientation. But beliefs are only important as they are perceived by the individual, and this is our major concern. The psychology of religion, as we have indicated, is primarily concerned with the individual's behavior. We have, however, spent some time on cultural factors because we recognize and appreciate the place of these factors in explaining the formation of religious beliefs.

H. Religious Beliefs and Behavior

The importance of religious beliefs lies in the fact that they often determine behavior. In themselves, beliefs may be static and lifeless. But they may also serve as motivating forces, driving man into a complexity of behavioral events. The beliefs which prompted Martin Luther to contradict the general principles of the Church were believed by many men and women before the Diet of Worms, but for some reason—or for many reasons—these beliefs forced the German monk to take a stand which did not guarantee safety to his physical self, but his action was necessary nevertheless in order to guarantee the integrity of his perceived self, thus achieving self-adequacy.

Certainly the average community contains groups of people having common beliefs but behaving differently. This is one of the salient problems of the psychology of religion, the relationship between beliefs and behavior.

SUMMARY

There are different levels of anlysis for understanding religious beliefs. A need system has certain limitations in that frequently need theorists resort to listing an assortment of "basic needs." It is suggested that a need for self-adequacy is a broad but useful postulate in understanding religious behavior, including religious beliefs.

Beliefs were defined as an enduring organization of perceptions and cognitions about some aspect of the individual's world. The more propriate a belief—that is, the closer it comes to one's self concept—the more like faith it becomes.

Beliefs have functional significance in that they assist in the satisfaction of man's need for adequacy.

We believe what we need to believe and only that. Beliefs, however, change due to the exigencies of life. There is a tendency to believe no more than is necessary in the establishment of self-organization.

Since religious beliefs may constitute a part of the self system, their intensity may be viewed in terms of their relationship to the self concept. The closer the religious beliefs come to the self concept, the more propriate they are. If, on the other hand, religious beliefs appear toward the outer layers, they are peripheral in nature. Actual influence on behavior may be measured in terms of geographical location in the self system. Those beliefs which have been internalized to the very core of the self system will determine behavior more than those beliefs assigned to outer areas of the self system.

However, the self system is dynamic in nature and religious beliefs may move inward and outward. This movement is partially determined by the success or failure of beliefs in satisfying the individual's need for self-adequacy. Those beliefs with high satisfaction value will tend to become propriate and part of the self concept itself; whereas those yielding little or no satisfaction of the basic need will be assigned peripheral positions away from the core of the self system.

Though culture furnishes and represents belief schema, the individual must perceive beliefs before they can determine behavior. The study of the perception and internalization of beliefs is one of the salient tasks of the psychologists of religion.

The importance of religious beliefs lies in the fact that they often determine behavior.

3
AFFECTIVE ASPECTS OF
RELIGION

A. The Religious Experience

The religious experience has been of continuous concern to the psychologist of religion. When we read the history of the psychology of religion we cannot help being impressed by the intense interest shown in this phenomenon. It is not an accident that the early psychologists of religion concentrated on religious experience, especially the conspicuous example known as conversion. For man must of necessity start with his experience. And the history of religion—even the history of theology—must start from the beginning, from the very bedrock of religious behavior, from the religious experience itself.

Though early writers agreed that the religious experience represents the focal point of our understanding, there agreement tended to cease. The very question, What is a religious experience? brought forth all kinds of possible explanations, from the unknowable *mysterium tremendum* of Rudolph Otto (1923) to the unresolved Oedipus

65

complexes of Sigmund Freud (1928). These explanations, along with all those in between these extremes, found followers and proponents. But the problem itself remains a central one in the psychology of religion.

B. Religious Experience as Perception

It is necessary in considering religious experience to make some observations about the psychological concept of emotion, for certainly emotion itself is an integral aspect of any religious experience. As Johnson (1959, p. 73) observes, "No experience is vital or dynamic without emotional support, and since religion is concerned with the deepest needs and highest worths of life, it will naturally be charged with emotional urgency."

Despite the fact that emotion has a long and prominent place in the history of psychology, it is impossible to offer an adequate definition of the term. Recent reviews of the concept indicate a wide assortment of meanings, but most of them admit the presence of heightened physiologic activities.

Our introductory psychology textbooks go to great pains to identify these physiologic changes. But what is not always made clear is that these purely physiologic reactions are the same in all experiences of an intense or propriate nature. Though we do not have a great deal of empirical data on the issue, we must assume for the time being that the bodily states of an individual having a religious experience are essentially the same as a person experiencing almost any other emotion. In other words, the bodily processes which occur under "emotion" are the same though the individual may describe the emotion he is experiencing in different ways.

Emotion, then, may be thought of as a kind of acceleration of certain body processes. Because body processes are always a part of the phenomenal field, these emotional reactions have a great deal to do with determining behavior.

In extreme cases body processes themselves may account for a large portion of the religious experience. Peyotism among the Navaho Indians is a marked example. The Peyote Cult is a semi-Christian religious movement with a ritual involving the consumption of the peyote cactus. The physiologic results of eating these cactuses are the same for different tribes, but it is the Navaho who "achieves communion with God," for the cognitive structure of the cultist includes the Christian God (Dittmann and Moore, 1957).

Since emotion then is in and of itself a kind of acceleration of body processes, it represents one aspect of the organism's search for self-adequacy. Whenever the organism perceives itself to be in a situation where there is a possibility of need satisfaction, emotional responses occur. In the same way, whenever the organism perceives itself to be in a situation which threatens the self, emotional reactions take place.

Obviously, the closer the perceived aspects come to the self concept the greater is the degree of emotional experience. When, for example, a picture of the Virgin Mary is perceived by the individual, it may or may not elicit an emotional response of some intensity. To the devout Roman Catholic the perceptional relationship to the phenomenal self may be propriate. In this case, the emotional response would be great. On the other hand, the same picture or statue to a Jew, or even another Roman Catholic where religious factors are peripheral, may elicit very little in terms of emotion.

Another item of considerable consequence is the appreciation of the distinction and relationship between emotions and feelings. Though the two terms are frequently used interchangeably, it is useful to make a distinction.

Whereas we have defined emotion as an acceleration of certain body processes, let us think of feelings as primarily *descriptions* of our perceptual fields at a particular moment. "Feelings are our perceptions of ourselves, of the situation in which we are involved, and the interrelationship of these two" (Combs and Snygg, 1959, p. 232).

Because of the complexity of our perceptual field, we frequently find it exceedingly difficult to describe our feelings. The history of mysticism clearly reveals the difficulty the great mystics had in describing their experiences. Undoubtedly, ineffableness is one of the salient characteristics of the mystic's experience. And it is little wonder, for in his attempt at describing his experiences he is faced with the tremendous task of stating in some shorthand fashion self perceptions, perceptions he has of God and nature, and the interrelationship of these.

We might well illustrate our point with a brief excerpt taken from an autobiographical report of an actual religious experience written by a young ministerial student, whom we shall refer to simply as John:

My call to serve came in a . . . wonderful and convincing way—it came from God! My own personal call came to me at L . . . during an M.Y.F. week's summer institute that had been so wonderful in its inspiration. Each evening vesper services were held. After a particular Thursday evening vesper service, it was suggested that we each practice solitary meditation and prayer. I went down by the side of the lake as the warm breeze from across the lake lapped the water on the pebbles and blew the light out of the sky so that the stars could be seen. Then in fading dusk where the beauty of the sky seemed in tune with the melody of the waves, God called me to harmonize my life with his by serving him. I remember hearing his voice. That evening I had a warm glow throughout that has never been repeated, although I have often wanted to recapture it.

Here we can get some idea of the complexity of the religious experience and of the difficulty involved in communicating the experience. This young man draws heavily on words of nature to express his feelings. This is quite common, for frequently the awe and magnificence of nature furnish an ideal set of factors to express profound feelings. Of course the perception of nature may stimulate or lead to the religious experience, but the perceiver must bring something to the encounter. After all, other young men and women certainly viewed that same lake and moon but with quite different responses.

We may examine the religious experience from a perceptual point of view by looking a bit closer at John's autobiographical statement. Since it is not an especially lengthy document, extensive excerpts are furnished the reader.[5]

In high school the most significant aspect of religious life to me was M.Y.F., even though I also attended Sunday School and Church. I enjoyed attending not only because the "popular" kids attended, but also because I found some of my personal problems answered. Furthermore, the minister's attraction at my home church drew heavily on me. I did admire and still highly respect practical intellectual knowledge and true manhood. These the minister combined with humor, personality, understanding, and a pleasant manner to be the most attractive individual in the community, at least for me. At every opportunity he encouraged me to enter the ministry and often invited me to his house for discussions.

Later on in high school I was picked out for leadership ability by the Hi-Yi members to be their president for three consecutive years. I enjoyed the opportunities for self-expression which I had in this service club. But being elected president of the local M.Y.F. and then district president was a great point in my life. They struck a deeper note in my life because M.Y.F. provided the deepest experience and highest definition of life that I could find anywhere.

What was this deep note? I think that in the words of the M.Y.F., I was desiring the highest

[5] This is one of several hundred autobiographical statements dealing with motivations for entering the ministry. Further analysis of these may be found elsewhere. Strunk, 1957b.)

kind of life because it was the most worth-while in terms of purpose, service, and friendships. I was convinced not only by the Christian interpretation of God, Jesus, and man, but also by the ministerial personnel and by the standard of character almost always to be found at youth meetings, especially those meetings on a district level.

These then were the ingredients of my call, but at the time I never recognized them as such. My call to serve came in a much more wonderful and convincing way—it came from God! My very personal call came to me at L . . . during an M.Y.F. week's summer institute that had been so wonderful in its inspiration. Each evening vesper services were held. After a particular Thursday evening vesper service, it was suggested that we each practice solitary meditation and prayer. I went down by the side of the lake as the warm breeze from across the lake lapped the water on the pebbles and blew the light out of the sky so that the stars could be seen. Then in fading dusk where the beauty of the sky seemed in tune with the melody of the waves, God called me to harmonize my life with his by serving him. I remember hearing his voice. That evening I had a warm glow throughout that has never been repeated, although I have often wanted to recapture it.

I was called in June. September of 1952 saw me enter the University to be enlightened, mostly self-enlightened. My first year at W . . . was not happy because my high-school sweetheart said good-bye, I had to study long hours, and I had to learn about all sides of human nature through a fraternity.

I not only learned about the other side of life, I practiced it too. Each year at college I became more secular, but friendships now gained a new depth and security for me. Gradually I began to doubt the validity of my call. The first two years I was not connected with any campus Christian association. In my junior year I served a rural community church that left me feeling fairly neutral in the service of that church itself. However, I enjoyed writing sermons, except when pressed for time, because they gave me a chance to do some theological thinking in practical terms.

.   .   .   .

The influence of the community of believers in Jesus Christ has played a central part in my personal development. Because of this, I know that it can do likewise in the lives of others. I feel strongly enough about this that I want to share in the vital work of the Christian Church.

Insidious reasons for my presence at seminary occasionally creep into my mind when I have those recurring periods of darkest doubt. They come in the form that I am in a rut by only being prepared to enter the ministry, or that I am cornered by previous commitments, or by the expectations of friends, ministers, and family, or by being in the ego-polishing position of leadership. But these feelings of sneaking in the back door of seminary are not predominant.

There are many facets of this brief account which will be of interest to us, but presently we are interested only in the religious experience itself. In an attempt to understand this experience it is necessary to analyze it in terms of John's perceptual field. We have noted that feelings are our perceptions of ourselves, of the situation in which we are involved, and the interrelationship of these.

In the case being noted, we can get some idea of John's self perceptions simply by reading his autobiographical statement. John sees himself as being a "man's man," an individual who needs to feel that he is a leader among men. Being elected president of the local Methodist Youth Fellowship was a significant point in his life. John's search for self-adequacy, therefore, found strong relationships in the religious area. That is, he was successful in achieving self-adequacy of his phenomenal self at an adolescent stage of development. The religious factors—M.Y.F. leadership and a philosophy of life having its foundation in "God, Jesus, and man"— partially satisfied John's need for self-enhancement.

Now let us place John beside the lake during a summer institute. What is the *situation?* We have noted already the physical factors present. But John perceives all of nature's beauty from a framework which pretty well had been laid long before that eventful evening. John was already "convinced" of the Christian interpretation of God, Jesus, and man. Indeed, not only are these religious factors part of his phenomenal field but "I-am-a-Christian-leader" is probably a factor bordering on the self concept itself. But surely by this time John has learned that a religious experience is a necessary pre-requisite to Christian leadership. Tentatively, one aspect of John's phenomenal field is "I-am-a-Christian-leader-without-a-religious-experience." It is this factor—coupled with hundreds of others—which makes up John's self perceptions.

In order for John—at this stage in his life—to achieve greater self-adequacy, he needs a religious experience. This he finds as his self perceptions come in contact with nature's marvels and as he interprets these marvels in the context of his Christian background. To simplify it, John's perceptions of himself—including the "I-am-a-Christian-leader-without-a-religious-experience"—comes in contact with a situation which produces emotional reactions, and the complex interrelation of these yields a unique feeling never again to be recaptured. This is John's religious experience.

To say that it is unique is obvious. Such an experience, by its very nature, must be unique in that it takes place in a psychological field of which there is only one. Nor will these unique relationships between the perceived self and the situation ever occur again. This is why John has never had *that* particular religious experience again though he has often "wanted to recapture it." John will not—indeed, can not—ever relive that particular experience again, for to do so would mean to reconstruct his psychological field as experienced at that particular moment. This is an impossibility because the religious experience itself is now a part of John's perceptual field. His self concept has changed. He is now "a-Christian-leader-with-a-religious-experience" and, quite spontaneously, this experience is interpreted as a call from God since he had previously learned the call concept.

Important to note is that this experience helped to stabilize, for a short time, John's perceptual field. Certainly up to this point John *valued* religious factors; they helped him to achieve self-adequacy. This experience brought these religious factors into a meaningful core of self perceptions. Religious factors such as the church, conversion, scripture, and so forth, have been made *propriate* for John. So much so, in fact, that they motivate him to enter college. Between the time of his religious experience and his first taste of college life, John's perceptual field was fairly stable, though certainly not static. Later, of course, other factors disrupt his perceptual field, but for a short time John found what he might have referred to as "peace of mind."

If we may return to our schematic diagrams for a minute (Figures 1 to 4), we may see that in the socialization process John learned an assortment of religious factors. These religious factors, taught to him in church and in church school, were part of his self system, though not really a part of his self concept. At the time of his religious experience, however, these factors were *internalized* (Figure 4). They penetrated to the very core of John's self concept; so much so that they *moved* him.

C. Temperament and Religious Experience

The reader at this point might well ask, Why John? Why should he have such a religious experience and not someone else? A partial explanation already has been given; that is, the fact of the socialization process. Early learning, attitudes, values, and so forth, are brought to the situation. It is not an exaggeration to say that literally hundreds of factors help to account for the religious experience.

But when these learned factors are identified and accounted for, there is still something missing. For such factors as church, doctrines, religious beliefs, attitudes, and values are learned by some but not by others. If we are to push the question far enough, we must at least give a nodding recognition to the role of temperament in determining the religious experience of an individual.

Unfortunately, temperament is another term which may mean many different things to many different people. It is necessary to give at least a general definition of the term as it is to be used in this discussion. Let us accept Allport's suggestions that temperament is a term which designates "a certain class of raw material from which personality is fashioned" (Allport, 1937, p. 53). It refers especially to dispositions that are almost unchanged from infancy throughout life.

There is practically no research whatsoever on the relationship between temperament and religiosity. Except for the conspicuous exception of W. H. Sheldon, American psychologists have tended to ignore or at least de-emphasize temperament as a variable determining behavior. But even in the case of Sheldon, the relationship of temperament and religiosity has not been examined carefully.

Leroy and Medakovitch (1929) have carried forth research which seems to tie certain heredity characteristics with a mystical propensity, but their research never has been extended and verified. Sward (1931) made a study in which he produced evidence which seemed to indicate that divinity students manifest more introverted tendencies than other individuals. But the primary instrument employed in this study was a self-rating scale, and there is serious doubt that Sward was measuring correlates of metabolic and chemical changes in bodily tissue. Parenthetically, the personality research tends to identify the professional religious person as the tender-minded, shut-in type of individual, though Strunk (1959b) discovered that preministerial students tend to be more socially aggressive than business administration majors.

It is safe to say that none of these studies really tackle the problem of temperament and religiosity unless we are willing to accept the various operational definitions of temperament at the expense of the more classical and literary connotations. But it is safe to say that the relation of metabolic factors as such to the religious experience has been hardly explored empirically.

Nevertheless, no one familiar with current research (e.g., Diamond, 1957) can ignore the possible role played by temperament. Within our perceptual orientation the concept loses its potency, but never should we ignore this area of concern. As was indicated previously, our perceptual field always includes our bodily processes. We have every right to believe, therefore, that temperament plays a significant part in explaining religious experiences, even though at present we have very little empirical evidence on the issue.

D. Forms of Religious Experience and the Self

The perception of environmental factors and bodily processes determine the individual's behavior. It is not surprising that religious experiences take

a variety of forms, especially when we realize that
no two perceptual fields are exactly alike. As one
reads the history of the psychology of religion he
cannot help wondering why a controversy should
arise over the possibility of *several* types of religious experience over against the view that there
is only one type of religious experience. The dis-
agreement partially can be understood when we
recognize that frequently the theoretical frameworks of critics were quite different, the one being
primarily *theological* and the other essentially *psychological* in nature.

It was William James's *Varieties of Religious Experience* which spotlighted the issue. This classical
volume made it perfectly clear that it is correct to
speak of religious experiences rather than *the* religious experience. James's final typology of religious
experience consisted of two major types, the "once-
born" and the "twice-born" person. James's analysis
is a useful one. It has been thoroughly elucidated in
several texts. We need not examine it carefully
here. It is sufficient to say that "sudden" religious
experience and the "gradual" religious experience
are helpful, descriptive categories, but like most
typologies they have a limited value in explaining
religious behavior. As Chein (1943) has amusingly
written, "the question of types is the staple pud-
ding of all psychologies because it gives everyone
a chance to put in his thumb and pull out a plum
and say: 'What a big boy am I.'"

Instead of becoming preoccupied with types of
religious experience, it would be better to consider
various *forms* of religious experiences; that is, pat-

terns of behavior which seem to be relatively common or frequent in occurrence.

Actually, there are as many forms of religious experience as there are perceptual fields. There are no two religious experiences exactly alike. A unique set of self perceptions comes in contact with a unique set of situational factors, the inter-relationship resulting in a unique perceptual field never again to be duplicated. In a sense, the internal factors and the situational factors yield an experience which is thoroughly unique. Thus it is that every religious experience is different from every other religious experience. It cannot be otherwise.

Nevertheless, such experiences have enough in common to permit us to speak of various forms of religious experience. We can, as we have already observed, identify at least two conspicuous and very broad forms which are somewhat analogous to the once-born and twice-born concepts.

Despite the oversimplification involved in this traditional identification, there is enough evidence in the literature to treat it with respect and to attempt to see these forms in perceptual terms.

The individual who grows into a religious person without any conspicuous and traumatic events gives the impression that a simple process is at work. But in actuality the process itself is highly complex. Briefly, the once-born person has consistently and smoothly internalized religious factors in either a highly differentiated way or in a partially differentiated way. Throughout most of his life this person has found religious factors quite satisfactory in his search for self-adequacy. To the external observer, this individual is able to sort and sift in such a way that there is very little conflict involved in the internalization process.

Under closer examination, it is frequently found that these people do experience internalization pains. There are times when religious factors conflict with one another or where nonreligious factors challenge religious factors. Despite these instances, however, this person *generally* finds that religious factors are *usually* capable of satisfying his need for self enhancement and self maintenance.

A careful reading of the following phenomenological report written by a young ministerial student illustrates this point well:

Like many children of the primary age there were days when I did not want to go to Sunday School, but my parents insisted and my older brother was willing to take me with him. As I look back I can see that a positive interest gradually developed. It was not brought about by the many sermons that I heard during those early years, for I couldn't understand them. I remember the parties we had and especially the festivities of the Christmas season. It was fun to receive a present from the church which was so willing to give, and it was fun to join in the joyous singing of carols. Everyone seemed so happy and friendly.

I distinctly remember when the realization dawned on me as to what the church actually was. My folks and I were going to a church supper one evening and as we neared the church I could see the shadows of people through the frosted window glass, busily working inside preparing the supper.

It suddenly came to me that those people were working because they wanted to, and because they loved their church and its people, even me. For the first time I knew what it meant to be a part of the church fellowship.

Later, when I became president of the M.Y.F., I discovered another great truth, and that is that when you are trying to live like Christ there is no such thing as your share of the Christian work to do. When you truly love God and wish to serve him to the best of your ability, you do all that you can do and you don't spend time worrying about what your share of the work is, neither do you become disgusted with the other fellow because he doesn't do as much as you do.

It was about this time that I realized how bad the Christian Church was in need of help. I saw situations in which I thought I could help. I saw areas that weren't being attended to. Someone had to help out in this work that needed being done. I felt that God was calling me to help Him in this great service. No longer could I satisfy myself by saying "let George do it." I felt that I ought to get into the work and contribute all that I could.

These were the days of decision, for I was not one to give myself all at once to the cause. Many occupations presented themselves to me. If God had stayed out of it I think I would have been satisfied without going to college, but God had called me and I was going to be a minister. The more I thought about it, however, the more I realized what a difficult job it would be. It was then that I decided to be an undertaker. I would be able to fool around in my work shop until the phone rang, and maybe I would have to work only three or four days a week in order to make enough to live very well. I planned to satisfy the desire to help other people by being a kind and understanding undertaker. I would even be able to give spiritual comfort to the mourners. There was to be a chapel where very meaningful funeral services would be held. I do not mean to say that undertakers have an easy time and make a lot of money, but that would have been my motive.

Later on I discovered that material things were not the most important contributors to happiness. God was persistent. He would not let me go. I decided once again that the ministry was for me. It wasn't long, however, before I again slipped away from Him. I didn't know what I was going to do but I wasn't going to serve in the thankless job of a minister. A minister does his best and the people kick him in the pants. Church people are supposed to be Christians, yet I had seen professed Christians do things that turned my stomach.

I was not to get away from God's grasp. He held on firmly and waited patiently. I soon realized that little misdeeds shouldn't discourage me because they were minor in the total ongoing of the Christian Church. One night as I lay on my pillow I gave myself to God during prayer. I surrendered my life to Him completely telling Him that I was ready to do whatever He wanted me to do.

Here I am starting seminary with plans for serving in the parish ministry. My motivations are those which have grown out of a steady growth. I want to take a ministry of friendship and love to the people that they may learn how to live the Christian life. So often we believe in Christianity but don't know how to live it. I know beyond doubt that God has called me to serve Him and I want to do as much as possible in His behalf. There is no share of work for me, I must do all that I can. I hope to encourage others to join the great fellowship in Christ that they may discover what I have discovered. I realize that I may not be able to do as great a task as I now want to do, but even if I accomplish a little, God will be pleased that I tried. Finally, there are important decisions for people to make. With God's help I may be able to help some make their decisions for Christ.

Here it is easy to observe a gradual and persistent growth, but it is also possible to note instances when non-religious factors invade religious ones. At one point the autobiographer actually makes a clear statement on this point: "These were the days of decision, for I was not one to give myself all at once to the cause." In an attempt to achieve self-adequacy, this man permitted another vocation to intrude into his self system. But this did not work. Already he had tasted the fruits of religious factors. He needed more, but there are nonreligious factors which might also give him a sense of self-adequacy. He experiments; but his self perceptions are such that he cannot be satisfied with anything less than total commitment to religious factors.

Though this total commitment was, as he himself notes, gradual, it was not a straight-line experience. There were crooks and bends in the road, but never once did he really move in a completely opposite direction. It is in this sense that we might with some validity refer to a "once-born" religious person.

Of course, the "twice-born" person has received the most attention in psychological literature. This it natural when we realize that these cases are often quite spectacular and conspicious. Most of the early studies of conversion were concerned with those persons who seemed to do "an about face," suddenly and dramatically. Though this form of religious experience does not seem to take place as much as it did at the turn of the century, the phenomenon is not unusual, especially in certain conservative denominations in the Bible Belt of the United States.

Psychologically speaking, the process involved in the sudden religious experience is the same as the gradual form of religious experience. That is, religious factors move from the periphery of the self system to the core, the self concept itself. The unique aspect is that this invasion appears to occur suddenly.

The following account is a rather unusual illustration of this form of religious experience. The subject is a middle-aged farmer who has just been converted. This excerpt, only slightly edited, is taken from a taped interview with the subject less than an hour after his religious experience:

SUBJECT: It's just too big . . . too joyful to talk about! I tried to tell Reverend Bell but I couldn't find the words. And I told Opal, I tried to . . . but . . . , I just can't; I tell you; it's just too big a thing, that's all.

INTERVIEWER: Well, Mr. Judson, can you give me some idea what happened?

SUBJECT: (Sighs heavily) I—I guess nobody will really get what I mean. I was . . . well, I was a

sinner all my life. I mean I was a *real* sinner. You
can ask anybody about Okey Judson. They'll tell
you I was the worst kind of devil. (Laughs) Ask
Opal! That poor woman put up with me for ten
years. She knows better than anyone about my
deeds of sin. Lord, but I can't understand how
that woman lived with me. Drinkin', smokin',
swearin', liein', carousin' . . . everything. . . .
And then this morning the Lord had his fill of
my sinful life.

I drove Opal to church, just like always. As I
was drivin' home, God spoke. I swear I was
surprised, but I *knew* it was God!! He just said,
"Turn around, Okey Judson, turn around." I
just shook my head, but I couldn't shake his
voice. He kept sayin', "Turn around, Okey Judson, turn around." And I turned that car around,
and there before me was an arch of lights over
the road . . . just as far as I could see was this
arch of lights. I drove right under it. I stayed
under it. Kept drivin'. I don't know how it happened but the next thing I recall was walking up
the aisle of that church, right up the center, right
up to Reverend Bell. And Reverend Bell, he was
just standin' there waitin'. Everybody seemed to
be expectin' me. They was smilin', and I could see
each and every one. . . I felt . . . well, I can't say
how I felt except that I loved them all. Everybody there loved me. I *knew* that!

To Mr. Judson this experience was sudden and
inexplicable. His phenomenological report indicates
a marked change in his perceptual field, and external
observers noted a radical reversal in his behavior.
Psychologically speaking, religious factors broke

into his self structure like a dam bursting forth with its tons of churning water. Though we do not have *sophisticated* evidence that Mr. Judson's self perceptions had changed greatly from before this experience to after it, reports of observers would lead us to believe that this most certainly happened.

We do have cases of religious conversion of persons while in psychotherapy (Bergman, 1953), of course, but "raw reports" like this one are difficult to come by.

Certainly from Mr. Judson's perceptual field, this experience is quite different from the experience described by the young ministerial student. But as we shall try to demonstrate in the next chapter, both are essentially the same in process; that is, both experiences are the result of a unique set of self perceptions coming in contact with a unique set of situational factors, the interrelationship resulting in a unique perceptual field—a field difficult to verbalize but one which nevertheless determines behavior.

E. Describing Religious Feelings

Feelings are the verbalizations of our perceptual field at a particular moment. In this sense, feelings are abbreviated descriptions of our perceptual field, and these feelings are essentially the result of an interrelationship of self perceptions and perceptions of the situation.

What makes feelings religious are the perceiver's interpretation and choice of symbols. Religious feelings, psychologically speaking, are defined by the perceiver. His perceptual field, which includes perceptions of historical events, perceptions of the contemporary situation, and perceptions of future plans, add or fail to add the religious interpretation.

1. Factors Determining the Description of Religious Feelings

Already we have demonstrated how differently religious feelings may be presented. John's autobiographical account of his spiritual development is rather sophisticated, whereas Farmer Judson's description is somewhat crude.

In the serious study of personal documents, we must appreciate such differences and understand the causative factors involved.

There are at least three general explanations for variation in describing religious experiences: vocabulary, the greater context, and the purpose of the description. Though it is not necessary to treat these factors at great length, their presence and power must be understood. Overlooking any one of these factors may lead to serious misunderstanding in judgments.

A) VOCABULARY

It may seem axiomatic to state that one's vocabulary is a significant variable in describing a perceptual field. But the communicative value of words is so important that we must constantly remind ourselves of it. Indeed, great variation in this variable may lead to serious misinterpretation on the part of the observer. In fact, variations may be so great as to suggest many "types" of religious experiences, when, in reality, quite similar experiences may be communicated in a radically different way.

The highly educated, verbally fluent individual trying to describe his perceptual field spontaneously draws upon his sophisticated vocabulary, whereas the near-illiterate, perhaps having an experience of equal intensity, may present a shorthand account which appears superficial to the observer. Actually, both persons seriously attempt to depict their phenomenal field—one, perhaps, in poetry, the other in crude, colloquial prose. We must not let vocabulary sophistication be the measure of the propriate or peripheral nature of the religious experience.

B) GREATER CONTEXT

Another factor—one of greater generality—we shall call greater context. Again, it may seem axiomatic, but a person's account of his feelings is greatly colored by the culture in which he stands and of which he is a part. A person brought up in a Christian environment does not express his religious experience in Buddhistic terminology. Nor does the Buddhist attempt to relate his experience in Christian jargon. These "foreign" factors are not part of the person's perceptual field, except, perhaps, in a peripheral sense.

The greater context, which is part of one's phenomenal field, helps determine the mode of expression. It cannot be otherwise.

Though we mention this factor only briefly, it should be remembered that sociologists and anthropologists have spent a great deal of study attempting to understand the implications of this factor. The brevity of the acknowledgment is not an assertion as to the importance or unimportance of this factor in understanding the religious experience. Our emphasis, however, stresses the *perception* of this greater context rather than the "real" content of it.

c) INTENTIONS

A third factor determining the nature of the report of a religious experience has to do with the *intentions* of the reporter. A person might wish to describe his religious feelings in hopes of converting others, in a desire to produce beautiful literature, in order simply to share the experience with others, and so forth. The individual's purpose will help determine exactly how the experience is to be handled.

Actually, vocabulary, greater context, and purpose are subconcepts in that they are all contained within the perceptual field itself. But these specifics are important and should be recognized and appreciated, for they determine the mode of expression which is what we, as external observers, hear and see and make inferences from.

F. Religious Feelings and Behavior

The description of religious feelings is important, but the fact that religious feelings lead to changes in behavior is the crucial concern of the psychology of religion. Though we shall concentrate on an analysis of observable acts in the next chapter, we can set the stage here by elucidating the theoretical relationship between the psychological field and behavior.

Our main proposition may be stated in simple terms: Changes in behavior are the direct result of changes in the perceptual field. The more radical the changes in the perceptual field the more conspicuous will be the changes in behavior.

Religious perceptions result in religious behavior. Obviously, at times the observable behavior may not be apparently religious, but this is only because the observer's field may not be even similar to that of the behaver's.

This may be amply illustrated in the case of the relationship between religion and politics. Frequently in discussing the subject of the separation of church and state people assume that this is the same as saying that religion and politics are separate entities, but this is a thoroughly ridiculous point of view. A field heavy with religious factors colors an individual's behavior. Indeed, it determines his behavior, including that type of behavior called "political." It cannot be otherwise.

If we turn to Figure 4 we can see this theoretical picture without effort. If the religious factors are strong in the psychological field and are deep—perhaps penetrating to the core of the self concept —the person is saturated with religious propensity. Most—perhaps all—of his behavior will be religious.

The more intense his religious feelings (perceptive field) the more intense will be his behavior.

SUMMARY

Despite the obvious complexity of the religious experience, it has occupied a central place in the psychology of religion. Though the religious experience is fraught with emotion; that is, bodily states of various sorts, it is more than emotion. The religious experience includes *feelings* which are descriptions of our perceptual fields at a particular moment. Because the religious experience is highly complex, it is difficult to describe and to communicate the exact feelings involved.

In an attempt to analyze the religious experience, psychologists have set up a dichotomy consisting of the gradual religious experience and the sudden religious experience. Though the division is a useful one, the psychological process itself is the same. In both forms, self perceptions come in contact with a situation, the relationship defining the religious experience. In the case of the gradual experience, the process is relatively mild and inconspicuous. In the case of sudden conversion, the influx of situational factors of a religious sort seemingly takes place in a short period of time. Both "forms" of religious experience create perceptual fields which determine behavior.

Religious experiences invariably depend on descriptions of such experiences. Three factors help to determine these descriptions: vocabulary, greater context, and the purpose of the relating of the experience. In reality, however, all of these are part of the individual's phenomenal field. In this sense, the description of the religious experience is a behavior resulting from the phenomenal field.

The relationship between religious feelings and behavior is direct. Changes in behavior are the result of changes in the perceptual field. The more intense the changes in the phenomenal field the more conspicuous will be the behavior of the individual.

4
CONATIVE ASPECTS OF RELIGION

A. Religion and Motivation

The influence of behaviorism in American psychology has been so intense that we naturally turn to observable behavior in our attempt at understanding. Though this exclusive and somewhat narrow approach has marked limitations in the study of religion, it is appealing and popular.

In this chapter we shall emphasize *behavioral acts* but in the context of our phenomenological orientation. As we have seen, thorough descriptions, objectively made, represent a first step in the understanding of psychological phenomena. The behavioral events discussed in this chapter—prayer, worship, ritual, and nonreligious acts—will be viewed as observable *events* to be studied and analyzed, but the perceptual orientation will be introduced and integrated in such a way that perception remains superior to the observable behavior.

Before examining specific behavioral acts, let us remind ourselves of the gross motive assumed to exist behind all such acts. It will be recalled that the basic need of human beings is to maintain and enhance the perceived self. Exactly how such behavioral acts as prayer, worship, and ritual accomplish this is our immediate concern.

B. Prayer

Prayer is an eminently good example of religious behavior. It is a good example because invariably the behaver perceives this activity as *religious*, and external observers are apt to agree with this classification. Thus it is that the psychologist of religion can claim this behavioral event as one province toward which he can direct his study.

Why do individuals pray? There is hardly any doubt that most people at some time in their lives pray. All questionnaire studies demonstrate this; but the *why* of the behavior introduces another dimension. That the motivational factor is highly complex has been demonstrated by an excellent empirical study conducted by A. T. Welford (1947). Using anecdotes as stimulus material, this worker had sixty-three subjects offer judgments as to whether they would pray or not in the specific situations described in the anecdotes in an attempt to discover if prayer is dependent upon affect or frustration. Statistical analysis of responses led Welford to the following conclusions:

1. Any simple hypothesis which regards prayer as a response merely to *distressing, threatening* forces is inadequate.

2. To some extent, a hypothesis which regards prayer as a response to *thwarting* or *frustration* ac-

counts for prayer, not only in unpleasant, but also in pleasant situations.

3. Neither frustration nor affect alone is adequate to account for prayer. Together they appear to account for a large part of the covariation in this experiment.

This study is important because it represents an attempt to verify or repudiate two theoretical positions dealing with religious behavior. According to J. C. Flower's (1927) theory any situation which presents features with which the individual is unable to deal adequately by means of existing reaction tendencies is clothed with images and analogies which aim at bringing it within the scope of these tendencies. Freud's theory (1928) simply states that religious behavior is a reponse to a particular environment which prevents adjustment in a normal manner. As Welford indicates in his conclusions, these theories are only partial explanations.

The study has another important facet to it since it demonstrates how our perceptual orientation can handle the behavioral event called prayer. Since prayer represents one form of behavior, we must say that it is a way the individual has found useful in achieving self-adequacy, in maintaining and enhancing the perceived self.

The affinity of this explanation to that of Flower's and Freud's is immediately obvious, but there are some important differences. Whereas Flower and Freud stress the frustrating nature of an encounter with a difficult environment, our phenomenological position stresses not only survival (maintenance of the self) but enhancement as well. It is undoubtedly true that the individual in difficulty (the self is threatened) will grab anything—perhaps even the practice of prayer, but what of the individual who finds himself secure and sound but nevertheless prays regularly?

The question again forces us to understand the quest of the pray-er: self-adequacy. An individual will pray and continue to pray so long as the behavior leads to maintenance and enchancement of the phenomenal self.

But how does prayer lead to self-adequacy? There are at least two ways:

1. *Prayer, as a reflective process, gives an individual a chance to evaluate himself in a relatively secure context.*

Though the adequate person perceives himself in generally positive ways, negative self attitudes often exist within the over-all organization of the phenomenal self. Defining relationships within the perceived self takes place in many situations and on various levels, but prayer offers a somewhat unique opportunity for self evaluations since it often eliminates many of the social stimuli which may color the evaluation.

Asking for things and giving thanks and confessing one's shortcomings may clarify the self concept sharply, thus leading to precise behavior. This is especially true with disciplined prayer where the individual makes praying an important part of his everyday life. The practice may assist him in codifying his self concept just as surely as his conversations and social interactions assist him to do this.

Even if prayer is "talking to one's self" the practice has psychological significance in that it provides
an excellent context for reflection and evaluation.

2. *Prayer provides an opportunity for extended
identification.*

The adequate individual is able to identify himself
with a great number of objects outside himself.
He is capable of extensive identification of self with
others. Prayer provides an opportunity for the widest kind of identification.

The ability for identification is undoubtedly
formed early in the socialization process. In the
very early years of life the organism is self centered
to an extreme degree but in the developmental process the child soon learns to invest himself in external objects. This process may begin within the
family context and slowly expand outward to include significant others, country, church, and so on.
If extension of the self is successful—that is, if it
leads to maintenance and enhancement of the perceived self—it will become a regular and valued
way of dealing with the world.

In prayer the opportunity for identification is
greatest in that the object is perceived as being the
most comprehensive and value-laden of all objects,
God himself. Obviously, the cognitive content of
the individual's faith partially determines the range
and depth of the degree of identification in the
prayer act. In some instances the prayer itself may
be centered on the verbalization of beliefs. If, for
example, the pray-er's intent is to consider the
brotherhood of man within the context of prayer,
he may achieve identification with all of mankind,

or perhaps even *all* objects, as in the case of certain religious mystics.

This opportunity for uninterrupted identification is determined, of course, by many variables but primarily by the degree to which it satisfies the need for maintenance and enhancement of the perceived self.

Prayer, then, is but a particular kind of religious behavior having as a psychological goal self-adequacy. And though we have stressed what the external observer might like to call "mature" or "disciplined" prayer, it must be recalled that the propriate nature of the prayer act, like all religious acts, is dependent on the pray-er's world. The public prayer of an ecclesiastical opportunist may be an *essential* act for self-adequacy even though the audience may generally perceive the superfluous string of words as strictly superficial and pedantic.

C. Worship

Much of what we have said about prayer is applicable to the religious act of worship, for here again, no matter the simplicity or complexity of the behavioral event, it is engaged in to satisfy the need for self-adequacy.

One writer (Johnson, 1957) has explained worship as an attempt for a finite person to complete himself within the context of a responsive relationship with Another. This is the interpersonal explanation for the fact of worship. We would rephrase the explanation a bit and claim that worshipful acts are an attempt to codify self perceptions. It may well be that this attempt is accomplished best when the worshiper faces what he perceives to be a third Person. This "looking glass" factor seem especially important in discussing worship, but it is really not necessary to get into the traditional argument over "objective" and "subjective" worship. Psychologically, the perception of the nature of the relationship is the significant factor.

It is the thesis of the phenomenological psychologist that the worshiper's perception of the nature of God does make a difference in the perceptual field and therefore in behavior. It is quite possible for a worshiper to go through all the movements but not believe in the existence of a Being outside himself. This is what traditionally has been called subjective worship. The other worshiper believes propriately that he is giving thanks or praise to an object external to him. Now the "subjectivity" of the first and the "objectivity" of the second depend completely on the perceptions of the worshiper.

It may well be—it is our "hunch" that it is so —that these perceptual differences have predictable concomitants in behavior, though we cannot at present offer concrete demonstrations.

The worship act, like the prayer act, has its power in its somewhat unique contribution to the maintenance and enhancement of the perceived self. If the individual perceives himself to be a good public worshiper and a faithful churchgoer, he will worship, even though he may not accept the implicit requirements of worship. Indeed, he might well be an agnostic; nevertheless, the public worship activity is needed by him and he will continue to use it so long as it satisfies his search for self-adequacy.

The psychological field of his neighbor, on the other hand, may contain the belief and feeling that he must approach, anticipate, praise, ask, offer, renew, and affirm to God whom he accepts in an I-Thou context. He may believe all this and feel all this in a propriate fashion and therefore the worship act is crucial in his achievement of self-adequacy.

But we must not forget that his neighbor who may go through the same acts of worship with the same vigor and consistency is doing so in order to impress his potential clients or to sell insurance or used cars. Worship to him, too, is propriate, but for entirely different reasons. Both are engaged in attempting to achieve maintenance and enhancement of the perceived self, but their self perceptions are quite different.

D. Ritual

Ritual has been defined as a prescribed form of activity, determined by considerations of tradition and symbolism. It is an important behavioral event in that it demonstrates the similarity in psychological fields and a general way in which the need for self-adequacy may be achieved. For a ritual is prescribed because it has proved itself. It works; if it ceases to work, it will be modified or discarded.

Rituals are codified behavioral acts which have satisfied the individual's search for self-adequacy over a long period of time. Through the learning process, man has discovered certain set ways which seem to agree with a significant portion of the population. These rituals give security and a sense of meaning to certain individuals, and they have tended to do so for generation after generation.

This would seem to imply that the individual with a strong need for patterned living will be drawn toward ritualistic religion. The exact relationship between religiosity and rigidity is not known though a few studies seem to indicate that the highly religious person is inclined toward general rigidity in personality.

Despite the lack of empirical evidence on this score, we do know that many religious practices, especially rituals, lend themselves to the individual in need of a relatively stable environment. On the elementary level we know that counting rosary beads *helps* some people in stressful situations. Now the counting of beads—that is, the act itself—may help an adult atheist or a devout Roman Catholic or a child not aware of the meaning of the act. In all three cases, however, the act is done in order to achieve self-adequacy, but only in the case of the Roman Catholic is it a *religious* act.

Ritual, whether it be the simple fingering of a rosary or the complex and symbolic activity of a High Mass, is primarily a well-established pattern of acts whose uniqueness rests in the general acceptability of these gestures in the search for self-adequacy.

E. Nonreligious Behavior

One of the most fascinating aspects of the psychological study of religion is the empirical establishment of specific relationships between religiosity and certain behavior not ordinarily called religious. This relationship may be in terms of the way in which the religious person behaves in the areas of politics, attitudes on social issues, interpersonal relationships, the handling of guilt, ethical behavior, and so on.

Over three decades ago Hugh Hartshorne and Mark A. May (1928) conducted an extensive study on the relationship between certain types of education and certain negative behavioral acts, such as cheating, lying, and stealing. The study is often used to demonstrate the lack of relationship between religiosity and character. This inference is usually made in light of one of the findings which indicated that children who attend Sunday school regularly cheat just as much as those who rarely or never attend Sunday school.

The jump from this conclusion to that of a stated relationship between religiosity and conduct is an immense one. The fact is that the Hartshorne-May study, significant as it is in the history of the psychology of religion and religious education, tells us absolutely nothing of the relationship between a psychological field filled with religious factors and behavior itself.

Indeed, there is not a single study in the literature which handles this problem explicitly and with sophistication. The scotoma implicit in all attempts at relating religiosity and behavior is the failure to appreciate and recognize the propriate and peripheral nature of religious factors and also the failure to take account of the behaver's unique field.

Our perceptual orientation, however, assumes certain relationships worth observing and worth consideration as fruitful hypotheses. We have reiterated the necessary relationship between the psychological field and behavior. We have even said that *all* behavior, without exception, is completely determined by, and pertinent to, the perceptual field of the behaving organism.

If the perceptual field is saturated with religious factors, as illustrated in Figure 4, then most or all behavior will be perceived as religious by the behaver. In Figure 4 we have an example of the person who has internalized a great deal of material of a religious nature, especially religious beliefs. So strong and so all-pervasive are these religious aspects that they seem to literally rule the individual in his everyday behavior.

This is the person who interprets *all* of life as a religious drama. His political views, his attitudes, his values—all are colored with the religious hue. For this person to talk about "non-religious" behavior is meaningless. Everything he does is a result of a psychological field packed with religious beliefs. Undoubtedly this type of person is so led by religious factors that explanation of his behavior in terms of a search for self-adequacy would be unthinkable.

O. Hobart Mowrer (1957) has made the insightful observation that one of the reasons the psychology of religion has floundered is that it makes a questionable assumption when it assumes that there is such a thing as the psychology of religion. Actually, it may be that religion itself is a psychology.

Surely the person depicted in Figure 4 is completely motivated by his basically religious field.

William J. Wolf (1959) in his excellent study of the religion of Abraham Lincoln has given us a literary picture of our theoretical position. Wolf observes:

Lincoln's religion cannot be hermetically sealed off from his social, economic, and political attitudes. His political action, as revealed by his own words, was ultimately the social expression of an understanding of God and of man that demanded responsible activity. This is contrary to a wide-spread modern opinion that religion should be a separate interest or even hobby in life and should not be allowed to influence fields like politics.

Perhaps the great mystics demonstrate even better the possible complete religious nature of the perceptual field, to the point where Brother Lawrence could perceive the washing of pots and pans as a basically *religious* activity bringing him into intimate contact with his god.

When we fully understand the basic differences between the perceptual field illustrated in Figure 2 and that in Figure 4, and also appreciate that responses on a questionnaire may be similar or alike in both of these instances, we know why it is that we are not in a position to make conclusive generalizations about relationships between religiosity and "nonreligious" behavior. The "objective" measures we have used to date invalidate, for the most part, our conclusions, and certainly bring into serious doubt the belief that we understand religious behavior at all.

SUMMARY

Prayer, worship, and ritual are behavioral events engaged in by individuals in an effort to achieve self-adequacy.

Prayer may lead to self-adequacy in two ways. First, as a reflective process it gives the person an opportunity to evaluate himself in a secure context. Second, prayer gives the individual a chance for wide identification. Both of these functions may be seen as "affirmative" results of prayer; however, the individual may also find prayer serving as a means of maintenance and enhancement within the area of social satisfaction. That is, praying publicly may be very important to the person even though God as an external Object may not be part of his psychological field.

Psychologically, worship and ritual are identifiable behavioral acts used to achieve self enhancement. The "objectivity" and "subjectivity" of worship are defined in terms of the perceptual fields of the behavers, the assumption being that the kind of perception of God will make a discernible change in behavior, though evidence for this assumption is lacking.

Though ritual serves the same purpose as prayer and worship, it has a special value in that it represents specific acts which have proven functional for many, thus eliminating experimentation in the desire for self-adequacy.

As to the relationship between the perceptual field saturated with religious factors and behavior called "nonreligious," we can only make the postulational observation that a religiously heavy psychological field makes *all* behavior religious, from the point of view of the behaver. In this instance, the behaver might talk of religion as motivation, so overpowering and complete is its effect. Despite the reality of this principle, the distinction between a perceptual field impregnated with religious factors and a field only spotted with religious factors has not been made in the traditional attempts at establishing relationships between religiosity and "nonreligious" behavior.

5
INTEGRATION

Our study of the way in which religious factors invade the psychological field and lead to behavioral events moves us to a general, systematic statement of one possible way we might take in our attempt to understand religion. At the same time, we will find it absolutely necessary to mention the limitations of our psychological position.

A. Religion, Problem-Solving, and Self-Adequacy

It is possible to look upon man as a problem-solving creature. From the moment of birth he is faced with a host of difficult situations or problems, and then, through hereditary and learned reactions, he attempts to meet these problems in a satisfying way. Though his specific problems are many in number, all are in reality a subdivision of one general and all-prevading problem: How to achieve self-adequacy.

At first he has available only the crudest kind of tools or factors to work with. He is severely handicapped by his very physical inadequacies. He must use other persons to achieve self-adequacy, especially parents and significant others. But as he matures, he learns to use symbols and signs, and these, along with other factors, serve him well in his never-ending search for self-adequacy.

But *self-adequacy means self-adequacy as perceived by the individual, thus producing a complexity.* For the person's self concept may be such that the simple, frequently physical aspects of the world are quite inadequate and unable to produce proper solutions to the basic and general problem. He is therefore forced to search and create, which leads him to the building and discovering of belief systems.

Many of these systems or factors—such as religious beliefs, prayer, religious acts, and so forth— the individual discovers accidentally as well as through deliberate training. He learns, frequently without clear differentiation (unconsciously), that certain religious factors solve certain problems admirably well. If this is the case, these religious beliefs are accepted and internalized so that for all practical purposes they become a part of the person. When his theology—the carefully worded statements describing religious factors—are thoroughly internalized we have a case of an individual's theology actually becoming the same as his psychology. Once internalized, and therefore propriate, these factors serve him continuously and adequately. If they should fail in the solving of the great problem-solving activity, they will be replaced with other types of systems.

B. Religion as a Comprehensive and
Integrating Force

There is a uniqueness about religious factors which is of special interest: Namely, they are frequently comprehensive.

The comprehensive nature of religious factors lies in the wide scope of methods made available to the individual's quest for meaning (self-adequacy). If, for example, the individual's self-adequacy depends upon an understanding of his beginnings and his destiny, he is more apt to find relevant factors capable of yielding answers in the religious area than in other areas; e.g., science, art, politics.

He may, of course, turn to these other systems, such as a group of scientific postulates, but if his self perceptions include a dimension which transcends the strictly physical, he will be disappointed. He may be forced to look further, and in his search he is apt to test and evaluate those religious factors which have been so thoroughly defined by countless generations of fellow searchers.

If he then finds these religious factors to be appropriate, he will hold to them and internalize them. In this sense, *religious factors always lead to integration of personality, for they obtain, one way or another, self-adequacy for the individual.*

This is difficult to accept when we look at the large number of studies seemingly dedicated to the thesis that religion leads to personality disintegration, neuroticism, and so on. But this is an external criticism which ignores the reality of the psychological field. The "neurotic" religious person —or for that matter the schizophrenic who seems oblivious to the external world—has often achieved self-adequacy through the use of religious factors, even though his society (and his doctors!) feel it necessary to institutionalize him because of his "odd" behavior.

But the religious factors *have* served their purposes. Our judgments and evaluations should not be of the religious factors, but of the particular kind of self perceptions demanding satisfaction, for *these* are the reasons for the adoption of the various behavioral events we as external observers see and judge and call "odd."

The argument, therefore, as to whether religion is "good" or "bad" for mental health is a hollow one, psychologically speaking. If religious factors are accepted and internalized they have shown their integrative power. The fact that the resulting behavior may be bizarre to the people outside the psychological field of the behavior is quite irrelevant. If, indeed, we could share the unique psychological field of the "odd" person, we would find that under the circumstances the religious factors have been successful in the problem-solving process.

Within the phenomenological context, religious factors are either not used (rejected) by the individual or they become integrative in nature.

C. Limitations of the Psychology of Religion

This perceptual or phenomenological position, like all truly psychological positions, implies a limitation which should never be overlooked by the student of religion. In the early days of the psycology of religion, E. J. Price (1924) wrote:

The psychology of religion, by its very nature as a science, is bound to restrict itself to a limited area of fact in order to explain it. In the total fact represented by the religious experience of prayer and conversion, psychology can take note only of the human, psychical side. The activity of God as such cannot become an object for scientific inquiry. Hence, the conclusions of psychology, as applied to religious experience, will be like all other scientific conclusions—true so far as they go, and within the limited area of the interest involved; but they are relative and not absolute. They need to be supplemented by and co-ordinated with other conclusions reached along philosophical and theological lines. The psychology of religion can never take the place of the philosophy of religion, nor can it render theology otiose. It can show us that religious experience is normal, and, by tracing the human mechanism of such experience, it may even encourage us to believe that the working of the normal mind, in this sphere as in others, may be trusted. It will still leave to the philosophy of religion the task of considering the final implications of such experience. Hence, while the mechanism of the psychology of religion may be granted for its own particular purposes, theology may still claim the right to consider the same facts under their divine aspect, so far as this lies open to us.

Unfortunately in the history of the psychology of religion and especially in the psychoanalytic study of religion, this warning frequently has been overlooked; and as a result we have accepted as final "truths" a great number of generalizations about religion which in reality are very limited in terms of view and method.

Our perceptual orientation to religion represents a postulational system with severe limitations. But these limitations may also be viewed as definite strengths in that the student may focus careful attention on his data and not become overpowered with the subtle complexities and tremendous scope of his subject matter. For if the student of religion insists upon seeing religion in all of its dimensions, he is faced with such a great domain that he cannot but stand helpless before his data.

Indeed, he would be forced into assuming the professional roles of not only psychologist, but anthropologist, historian, sociologist, philosopher, theologian, *ad infinitum*. For religion does consist of all these dimensions and perhaps more. Systematic study along all these lines at the same time and by a single person is an utter impossibility.

It therefore becomes necessary to work within a rather stable postulational system, such as the one described in this volume—always remembering, of course, the limitations of the approach when making generalizations about religion.

For some persons such an approach to an understanding of religion may be unbearable. To these persons theology or philosophy may be in a better position to handle the particular kind of questions in need of answering. This is fine and the way it should be.

But before dismissing the perceptual approach to the understanding of religion the student should remember that any religious factor—even the most basically theological kind—may enter the psychological field of an individual and therefore becomes a datum for investigation. He is then free to attempt to understand that theological statement within the psychological context. It is true he cannot and should not make generalizations about the ultimate truth or falsity of that statement, but he can and should understand its significance in determining behavior. This, it would seem, is a noble task.

A theologian recently said, after being personally involved in a serious social crisis, "I have learned one thing from this terrible experience: When the going gets rough and the chips are down, a person doesn't respond to the situation in terms of his theology but in terms of his psychology."

We must add, however, that his theology might be internalized—sent to the very core of the self concept—so that his theology becomes his psychology and will determine his behavior.

This internalization process and its resulting effects are the data of the psychologist of religion. The student dedicated to the understanding of even these limited areas has a complex task. Later, perhaps, if he does his job well, theology and philosophy may give sound and general interpretations and generalizations about the religious. But both theologian and philosopher will need the kind of data which can only be uncovered through the phenomenological search.

SUMMARY

Man, as a problem-solving creature, has as his major problem the achievement of self-adequacy. In order to solve this problem he makes use of many factors, some of which may be religious in nature. If religious factors are successful, he will internalize them and continue to find them useful in his dealing with the world. It is in this sense that religion is always an integrating force, though it may not appear so to the external observer who does not share the same psychological field with the religious person.

Religious factors frequently serve individuals better than other systems of factors because they give answers to the most extensive kind of questions asked by man.

The phenomenological or perceptual study of religion has limitations like all specialized attempts at understanding. Though it cannot make sound generalizations as to the validity or falsity of religious propositions, it can attempt to understand theological statements when they enter the psychological field of individuals.

If the psychologist of religion does his job well, he can be of invaluable aid in furnishing data to the theologian and philosopher whose task it is to understand religion in its widest and most ultimate context.

REFERENCES

Adler, A. 1933. "Religion und Individual-psychologie." In Ernst Jahn and Alfred Adler: *Religion und Individualpsychologie; eine prinzipielle Auseinandersetzung über Menschenführung.* Vienna, Leipzig: Rolf Paeser.

Allport, Gordon W. 1937. *Personality: A Psychological Interpretation.* New York: Holt, Rinehart & Winston.

———. 1943. "The Ego in Contemporary Psychology," *Psychological Review,* L, 451-78.

———. 1950. *The Individual and His Religion.* New York: The Macmillan Co.

———. 1955. *Becoming.* New Haven, Conn.: Yale University Press.

Ames, E. S. 1910. *The Psychology of Religious Experience.* Boston: Houghton Mifflin Company.

Bergman, P. 1953. "A Religious Conversion in the Course of Psychotherapy," *American Journal of Psychotherapy,* VII, 41-58.

Beth, K. 1930. "Aufgabe und Method in der Religionspsychologie," *Zsch. f. Religionspsychologie,* III, 5-12.

Bills, R. E. 1959. "Believing and Behaving: Perception and Learning." In A. Frazier (Ed.), *Learning More About Learning*. Washington, D.C.: National Education Association.

Blacker, C. P. 1946. "Galton's Outlook on Religion," *Eugenics Review*, XXXVIII, 69-78.

Boozer, J. 1960. "Comments on 'Religion, the Id, and the Superego,'" *The Journal of Bible and Religion*, XXVIII, 323-28.

Boring, Edwin G. 1950. *A History of Experimental Psychology*. New York: Appleton-Century-Crofts, Inc.

Brown, Clarence W., and Ghiselli, E. E. 1955. *Scientific Method in Psychology*. New York: McGraw-Hill Book Co. Inc.

Brown, W. 1925. "Religion and Psychology," *Hibbert Journal*, XXIII, 402-17.

Chein, I. 1943. "Personality and Typology," *Journal of Social Psychology*, XXVIII, 89-109.

Clark, Walter Huston. 1958. *The Psychology of Religion*. New York: The Macmillan Co.

Combs, Arthur W., and Snygg, Donald. 1959. *Individual Behavior*. New York: Harper & Brothers.

————, and Soper, D. W. 1957. "The Self, Its Derivative Terms, and Research," *Journal of Individual Psychology*, XIII, 134-45.

Cronbach, A. 1926. "Religion and Psychoanalysis," *Psychological Bulletin*, XXIII, 701-13.

————. 1928. "The Psychology of Religion. A Bibliographical Survey," *Psychological Bulletin*, XXV, 701-19.

Cunningham, E. C. 1956. "Postulational Systems: Gateways to Understanding," *Educational Theory*, VI, 47-59.

Diamond, Solomon. 1957. *Personality and Temperament*. New York: Harper & Brothers.

Dittmann, A. T., and Moore, H. C. 1957. "Disturbance in Dreams as Related to Peyotism Among the Navaho," *American Anthropologist*, LIX, 642-49.

Dreger, R. M. 1952. "Some Personality Correlates of Religious Attitudes as Determined by Projective Techniques," *Psychological Monographs*, 66.

Dudycha, G. J. 1930. "The Religious Beliefs of College Freshmen," *School and Society*, XXXI, 206-8.

———. 1950. "The Religious Beliefs of College Freshmen in 1930 and 1949," *Religious Education*, XLV, 165-69.

Dunlap, K. 1946. *Religion: Its Functions in Human Life*. New York: McGraw-Hill Book Co., Inc.

England, R. W. 1954. "Some Aspects of Christian Science as Reflected in Letters of Testimony," *American Journal of Sociology*, LIX, 448-54.

English, Horace B., and English, Ava C. 1958. *A Comprehensive Dictionary of Psychological and Psychoanalytical Terms*. New York: Longmans, Green & Co., Inc.

Fahs, Sophia L. 1930. "The Beginnings of Religion in Baby Behavior," *Religious Education*, XXV, 896-903.

Flower, John Cyril. 1927. *An Approach to the Psychology of Religion*. Harcourt, Brace, & Co., Inc.

Freud, S. *Collected Papers*. Hogarth Press, Ltd. 5 vols.

———. 1928. *The Future of an Illusion*. Hogarth Press, Ltd.

Fromm, Erich. 1950. *Psychoanalysis and Religion*. New Haven, Conn.: Yale University Press.

Gillespie, J. M., and Allport, G. W. 1955. *Youth's Outlook on the Future*. New York: Doubleday & Company, Inc.

Goldstein, Kurt. 1939. *The Organism*. New York: American Book Company.

————. 1940. *Human Nature in the Light of Psychopathology*. Cambridge: Harvard University Press.

Hall, C. S., and Lindzey, G. 1957. *Theories of Personality*. New York: John Wiley & Sons, Inc.

Hartshorne, Hugh, and May, M. A. 1928. *Studies in Deceit*. New York: The Macmillan Co.

Henle, Mary. 1957. "Some Problems of Eclecticism," *Psychological Review*, LXIV, 296-305.

Hiltner, Sewart. 1947. "The Psychological Understanding of Religion," *Crozier Quarterly*, XXIV, 3-36.

Hopkins, P. 1937. "A Critical Survey of the Psychology of Religion," *Character and Personality*, VI, 16-35.

James, William. 1903. *Varieties of Religious Experience*. New York: Longmans, Green & Co., Inc.

Johnson, E. H. 1943. "Personality Traits of Workers in the Field of Religion," *Religious Education*, XXXVIII, 325-29.

Johnson, P. E. 1951. "Psychology of Religion," *Journal of Bible and Religion*, XIX, 25-27.

Johnson, Paul E. 1959. *Psychology of Religion*. Nashville: Abingdon Press.

Jones, E. 1926. "The Psychology of Religion," *British Journal of Medical Psychology*, VI, 264-69.

————. 1944. "The Psychology of Religion," in Sandor Lorand (Ed.), *Psychoanalysis Today*. New York: International Universities Press, Inc.

Jung, Carl G. 1933. *Modern Man in Search of a Soul*. New York: Harcourt, Brace and World Co.

————. 1938. *Psychology and Religion*. New Haven, Conn.: Yale University Press.

————. 1958. *Psychology and Religion: West and East*. New York: Pantheon Books, Inc.

Kortlandt, A. 1955. "Aspects and Prospects of the Concept of Instinct," *Arch. Neerl. Zool.*, XI, 155-284.

Krech, David, and Crutchfield, Richard S. 1948. *Theory and Problems of Social Psychology*. New York: McGraw-Hill Book Co., Inc.

Landsman, T. 1958. "Four Phenomenologies," *Journal of Individual Psychology*, XIV, 29-37.

Lawton, G. 1930. "The Psychology of Belief," *Psyche*, X, 73-82.

Leroy,—,and Medakovitch,—. 1929. "Delire Mystique Chez deux Jumeaux," *Annales Medico-psychologiques.*

Leuba, James Henry. 1912. *A Psychological Study of Religion*. New York: The Macmillan Co.

Lewin, Kurt. 1935. *A Dynamic Theory of Personality*. New York: McGraw-Hill Book Co., Inc.

————. 1936. *Principles of Topological Psychology*. New York: McGraw-Hill Book Co., Inc.

————. 1951. *Field Theory in Social Science: Selected Theoretical Papers*. New York: Harper & Brothers.

Lundeen, G. E., and Caldwell, O. W. 1930. "A Study of Unfounded Beliefs Among High School Seniors," *Journal of Educational Research*, XXII, 257-73.

Maslow, A. H. 1954. *Motivation and Personality*. New York: Harper & Brothers.

Mowrer, O. Hobart. 1957. "Some Philosophical Problems in Psychological Counseling," *Journal of Counseling Psychology*, IV, 103-11.

————. 1959. "The Unconscious Re-examined in a Religious Context." In Orlo Strunk, Jr. (Ed.),

Readings in the Psychology of Religion. Nashville: Abingdon Press.

Müller-Freiennfels, R. 1935. *Evolution of Modern Psychology.* New Haven, Conn.: Yale University Press.

Murphy, Gardner. 1958. *Human Potentialities.* New York: Basic Books, Inc.

Murray, Henry A. *et al.* 1938. *Explorations in Personality.* New York: Oxford University Press.

Nelson, M. O., and Jones, E. M. 1957. "An Application of the Q-Technique to the Study of Religious Concepts," *Psychological Reports,* III, 293-97.

Niebuhr, R. 1955. *The Self and the Dramas of History.* New York: Charles Scribner's Sons.

Oppenheimer, O. 1958. "Toward a New Instinct Theory," *The Journal of Social Psychology,* XLVII, 21-31.

Orr, F. C. 1955. "The Psychology of Religion: I. A Review of the Literature. II. A Study of Client Religious Sentiments as Related to First Interview Counseling Behavior." Unpublished Doctor's Dissertation, University of Missouri.

Otto, Rudolf. 1923. *The Idea of the Holy.* London: Oxford University Press.

Page, F. H. 1951. "The Psychology of Religion After Fifty Years," *Canadian Journal Psychology* V, 60-67.

Pratt, J. B. 1908. "The Psychology of Religion," *Harvard Theological Review,* I, 435-54.

Price, E. J. 1924. "The Limitations of the Psychology of Religion," *The Hibbert Journal,* XXII, 664-73.

Rank, Otto. 1950. *Psychology and the Soul.* Philadelphia: University of Pennsylvania Press.

Rogers, Carl R., and Dymond, Rosalind F. (Eds.) 1954. *Psychotherapy and Personality Change.* Chicago: University of Chicago Press.

Schaub, E. L. 1922. "The Present Status of the Psychology of Religion," *Journal of Religion,* II, 362-79.

——. 1926. "The Psychology of Religion," *Psychol. Bull.,* XXIII, 681-700.

——. 1926a. "The Psychology of Religion in America During the Past Quarter-century," *Journal of Religion,* VI, 113-34.

Starbuck, E. D. 1903. *Psychology of Religion.* New York: Charles Scribner's Sons.

Stephens, John M. 1951. *Educational Psychology.* New York: Holt, Rinehart & Winston.

Stephenson, William. 1953. *The Study of Behavior.* Chicago: University of Chicago Press.

Strunk, O., Jr. 1955. "Motivational Factors and Psychotherapeutic Aspects of a Healing Cult," *Journal Pastoral Care,* IX, 213-20.

——. 1957. "The Present Status of the Psychology of Religion," *Journal Bible and Religion,* XXV, 287-92.

——. 1957a. "A Redefinition of the Psychology of Religion," *Psychological Reports,* III, 138.

——. 1957b. "Men, Motives, and the Ministry," *Religious Education,* LIV, 429-34.

——. 1958. "The Psychology of Religion: An Historical and Contemporary Survey," *Psychological Newsletter,* IX, 181-99.

——. 1959. *Readings in the Psychology of Religion.* Nashville: Abingdon Press.

——. 1959a. "Perceived Relationships Between Parental and Deity Concepts," *Psychological Newsletter,* X, 222-26.

——. 1959b. "Interest and Personality Patterns

of Preministerial Students," *Psychological Reports*, V, 740.

Sward, K. 1931. "Temperament and Religious Experience," *Journal of Social Psychology*, II, 374-96.

Takenaka, N. 1939. "The Motive of Religious Interest in Children Living Near the Sea," *Japan Journal of Psychology*, XIV, 251-54.

Talbert, E. L. 1933. "On Francis Galton's Contribution to the Science of Religion," *Scientific Monthly*, XXXVII, 205-49.

Thouless, R. H. 1935. "The Tendency to Certainty in Religious Belief," *British Journal of Psychology*, XXVI, 16-31.

Trout, D. M. 1931. *Religious Behavior*. New York: The Macmillan Co.

Uren, Albert Rudolf. 1928. *Recent Religious Psychology*. New York: Charles Scribner's Sons.

Warren, Howard Cosby. 1934. *Dictionary of Psychology*. New York: Houghton Mifflin Company.

Welford, A. T. 1947. "Is Religious Behavior Dependent Upon Affect or Frustration?" *The Journal of Abnormal and Social Psychology*, XLII, 310-19.

Wolf, William J. 1959. *The Almost Chosen People*. New York: Doubleday & Company, Inc.

Wundt, W. 1902. *Facts of the Moral Life*. New York: The Macmillan Co.

———. 1916. *Elements of Folk Psychology*. New York: The Macmillan Co.

INDEX

0(